BAPTISM OF FIRE

Forthcoming Works from Great Northern Publishing

Non-Fiction:
Bombardment! - WWI
The War Of The Yorkshire Gurkhas - WWI

Fiction/Adult Humour:
Hazardous to Health - An Obadiah Jones Novel
Under Surveillance - An Obadiah Jones Novel
A Bridge Too Far - An Obadiah Jones Novel
An Alien Affair

Science Fiction/Adult Humour:
Beyond The Void - An Erasmus Novel
The Love Colony - An Erasmus Novel
Howling At The Moon - An Erasmus Novel
Montana Springs

Western/Adult Humour:
Bitter Creek

Adult Fiction:
Dark Passions - Anthology
My Soul To Keep - Anthology
Intimate Strangers

Fantasy Humour:
Poddrantallingtondibble - In Search of Odenhall
Poddrantallingtondibble - Homeward Bound
Granny Capstick

Fantasy:
The Book Of Dale

Fiction/Childrens:
Teddy Buttons
A Time To Wish

BAPTISM OF FIRE

An account of the 5th Green Howards
at the Battle of St Julien,
during the Second Battle of Ypres,
April 1915.

MARK MARSAY

GREAT NORTHERN PUBLISHING

BAPTISM OF FIRE
An account of the 5th Green Howards at the Battle of St Julien, during the Second Battle of Ypres, April 1915.

Part One of 'The War of the Yorkshire Gurkhas' series.

ISBN: 0 9535204 0 4

Cover illustration: reproduced courtesy of The Green Howards Regimental Museum, Richmond, North Yorkshire

First published by Great Northern Publishing 1999.

GREAT NORTHERN PUBLISHING
PO Box 202
Scarborough
North Yorkshire
YO11 3GE

Printed and bound by
Redwood Books
Trowbridge
Wiltshire

Private James Richard Stevenson MM
14th May 1895 to 26th May 1996
'Remembered with pride - never forgotten'

Contents

From the foreword to The History of the 50th Division

There is a carved screen in Newcastle, entitled **'The Response'**, which vividly recalls the magnificent reply of the North when the call came in 1914. This response was in keeping with the history of the North of England which, for many centuries, had known the necessity of being responsible for its own defence.

Some may have had doubts as to whether, when the test of war came, the Territorial Force would prove itself equal to the Regular battalions of the Army.

The first test came a few days after the Division landed in France, at the battle of St Julien, and the Division had few harder battles during the war. During the first two days each of its three Infantry Brigades (149th, 150th, 151st) fought in turn over the ground where the 50th (Northumbrian) Division Memorial now stands, and during this action made that reputation for hard fighting which it maintained throughout the war.

Major-General Sir Percival S. Wilkinson
Officer Commanding 50th (Northumbrian) Division
5th August 1915 to 24th February 1918

Author's Introduction

In the course of preparing a much larger work, based on the diaries, papers and memories of my Grandfather, Jim Stevenson MM, dealing with the whole detailed story of the 5th Green Howards during the Great War, I have gathered so much information that not all of it can be included.

Therefore, as there is an abundance of material relating to the very first action the Battalion saw on the Western Front, the majority of it written by the men who were there, I feel I should set what I can down on paper, thereby allowing those men to help me tell their story in their own words. Though I have taken to highlight, in the main, the Scarborough men of the Battalion, this is in no way meant to detract from the equally deserving men who served from the other towns and villages about the region - it is simply because the bulk of the writing available to me is Scarborough based.

My Grandfather died, aged 101, in May 1996 and was the very last surviving member of the *'original'* 5th Battalion; those Territorials who landed in France in April 1915. Throughout the war he maintained a daily diary, even after being taken prisoner in May 1918, and it is this which forms the basis of the greater work under preparation.

It should be noted that I am fully aware the Regiment was officially designated as **Alexandra, Princess of Wales's Own Yorkshire Regiment** (or known simply as the Yorkshire Regiment) at that time. However, I refer to the Regiment throughout as the **Green Howards** (which designation was officially approved in 1920) because my Grandfather always, without fail, referred to himself as such - ***'A Green Howard, and proud of it'***.

Having got to know men of the Regiment in the course of my research, and counting many among them as friends, I now understand a little better what it means to them to be Green Howards, and so use the title in my work as a mark of respect.

With regard to the title of the Division, I have opted to use the designation of the 14th May 1915 (coincidentally, my Grandfather's birthday), of **'50th (1st Northumbrian) Division'** [which is often shortened in the text to the 50th Division] to avoid confusion by suddenly changing from *'1st Northumbrian Division'*, which it was while at home, to the *'50th (1st Northumbrian) Division'* which it was when on active service, having adopted the Regular Army system of numbering divisions.

This work is not intended to be an academic tome, rather the narrative is intended to provide the reader with a guide, a platform if you will, from which to view, in context, the letters and verse of the men who are mentioned in its passages.

It should be noted that I have endeavoured to give an accurate chronological account of events. In some instances this has proved somewhat difficult because of the contradictions and conflicting nature of various research materials (unit diaries, personal diaries, official histories etc.) - but none of these discrepancies are of a major nature and I hope that by combining several accounts, a single, 'viable' one is the result.

For any errors or omissions I apologise, and if appraised of them will endeavour to correct them in subsequent works.

I would also like to apologise for the quality of some of the photographs used, many taken from microfiche, but because they are an integral part of the work I felt they should be included nonetheless.

I should perhaps emphasise here, though it has already been mentioned, that the 5th Green Howards was a **Territorial** unit - as were all those in the 50th (Northumbrian) Division. I reiterate this fact because I feel it is important for the reader to be able to differentiate between these so called ***'Saturday Night Soldiers'*** and the formation of the Kitchener New Armies (the *Service* and *Pals'* battalions).

The Territorial Force had long been an object of ridicule among the older and unenlightened members of the military 'establishment' and even Kitchener himself (a Cavalry officer, not an infantryman) had little time for them. However, it is worthwhile to note that these Saturday Night Soldiers produced more infantry battalions than either the Regular Army or Kitchener's New Army. Despite this there has generally been more made of, and written about, the heroic and stalwart Regulars of 1914 and the waves of the slaughtered innocent Kitchener battalions on the Somme in 1916, than of the dogged and determined Territorials. It is perhaps therefore appropriate, at the beginning of this book, that I leave the last word about the Territorials to two of those Saturday Night Soldiers' well-known contemporaries:

> *The Empire will never forget the inestimable services rendered by Territorial Troops throughout the Great War, more especially during those early and critical days before the New Armies were ready to take the field. The gallantry and self-sacrifice of the men who fought and fell will be an inspiration for all time.*
> [King George V speaking in 1929, on the 21st Anniversary of the Territorial Army's formation.]

> *Equally distinct were the Territorials from what has been called the New Army, whose officers and men had ample time to prepare themselves for what they were required to do. I sometimes wonder if the eyes of the country will ever be open to what these Territorial soldiers of ours have done.*
>
> *I say, without the slightest hesitation that, without the assistance which the Territorials afforded between October 1914 and June 1915, it would have been impossible to have held the line in France and Belgium, or to have prevented the enemy from reaching his goal of the Channel seaboard.*
> [Field Marshal Viscount French of Ypres in 1919.]

It is in honour of my Grandfather's service, and for his providing me with the incentive and inspiration to write, that I dedicate this book to his memory.

Preface

I first met Mark in April 1996 when I was among a group of Green Howards making a presentation to his grandfather, Jim Stevenson MM, one of the last survivors of the Somme Battles of 1916. We talked at length and I was shown Mark's work based on his grandfather's diaries, papers and memories - a work covering the Great War from Jim's perspective and that of the 5th Battalion Green Howards. Mark, rather wisely, decided to precede his major work with several smaller books, each dealing with a particular aspect of the Great War on which he has gathered an abundance of material. This is the first of those books and I was surprised, but pleased, to be asked to write the preface for it.

~

At 5.00pm on 22nd April 1915, a series of thick plumes of greenish smoke were seen drifting from the German trenches south-west towards the French-held positions around Ypres. It was the first time chlorine gas had been used in the Great War. By 7.00pm, all roads to the rear were clogged with transport and terrified French soldiers choking and gasping for air. Twenty-four German battalions poured through the gap left by the fleeing troops and established themselves on bridgeheads along the Yser Canal. The situation for the British High Command was desperate. Fortunately, the flanking Canadians had stood firm. Yet urgent measures were now needed to plug the gap and the 50th (Northumbrian) Division was ordered to the front to support the Canadians and counter-attack the German advance.

So it was that on St George's Day 1915, the Battle of St Julien began and with it the baptism of fire for the men of the 5th Green Howards. These young men from the north-east coast had volunteered to serve overseas, and although they had trained hard in England since the outbreak of war, they had only just arrived in France, still equipped with outdated equipment and ineffective Lee Enfield Mark 1 rifles. Most of the men were in their early twenties and many had never left Yorkshire before. Nor had they ever experienced the mind-numbing effects of an artillery barrage or been subjected to the impact of machine-gun fire. Yet these volunteers belonged to a proud County

Regiment with a long history; many of their fathers and grandfathers had served in the Green Howards. They were Territorials, who felt themselves to be just as good as the Regulars and they were not going to let their families or their Regiment down. It was in this spirit they marched to the front.

Through a gripping narrative, based on official records of the battle, supported by the personal letters, diaries, poems and archive photographs of the men themselves, Mark tells the story of how these young men faced their baptism of fire with extreme courage and tenacity. He recounts how they fought for the next seven days on a diet of bully beef and biscuits, sometimes sipping water from the puddles in the bottom of their hastily constructed trenches. He tells how they faced barrage after barrage of German artillery fire which not only destroyed but also prevented any resupplies being brought up from the rear.

It was the 5th Green Howards' first action and they suffered terribly. Yet they advanced to fill the gap and support the Canadians, and together they stopped a full-scale German breakthrough and sealed the broken front line.

It was this first action which earned the 5th Green Howards the nickname the 'Yorkshire Gurkhas' - a mark of respect from their front-line colleagues. After they were relieved, the Commander-in-Chief of the British Expeditionary Force, Sir John French, personally expressed his admiration of the behaviour of the Battalion to the assembled survivors (the speech is reproduced in its entirety later in the book). Indeed throughout the war they were called upon continually and played their part in every major battle on the Western Front until disbanded late in 1918. Despite everything the war would bring to them, few other engagements could compare to the Battle of St Julien - which was to be, for the 5th Green Howards, their first Battle Honour of the Great War and their ***'Baptism of Fire'***.

I highly commend this work to Green Howards, students of military history and the people of Yorkshire and the north-east.

Major J. Roger Chapman, MBE
The Green Howards Regimental Museum, Richmond
February 1999

~

Twice since have they been in action
And wrought some glorious deeds;
But the one which was fought at St Julien,
Was where they proved more than weeds.

~

Taken from the poem
'The Gallant Fifth Green Howards'
by Private James Brough

Postcard of the period;
'The barbarous Hun despoiling Belgium in 1914'

BAPTISM OF FIRE

The 5th Green Howards at the Battle of St Julien, during the Second Battle of Ypres, April 1915

It had been a long haul. For many of the old-hand Territorials it had begun at the outbreak of war in August 1914, when the 5th Battalion, then at annual camp at Deganwy Camp in Wales, was called to active service. Both new recruits and former Terriers (Territorials) rushed to enlist in their local Battalion and had quickly swollen its ranks, bringing the 5th Green Howards up to fighting strength.

The early days of training for these fresh-faced young recruits had taken place in their local towns and drill halls, the places of enlistment. Daily they could be seen mustered, paraded and then marched to and fro in fields and streets; parades and drills, drills and parades. Within a matter of weeks those first volunteers were shipped off to join the main body of the original 5th Battalion, already training hard at Darlington. Eventually they found their way to Newcastle, the northern base for the assembly of the 50th (1st Northumbrian) Division, there to finish their preparations.

All the while the war went on without them.

After the first heady rush of volunteers had enlisted, in the frenzied days following the Battalion's embodiment for war, a frustratingly long wait to get to the front ensued. The thwarted men of the 5th Battalion were left champing at the bit and grumbling among themselves. Some thought they might never see action at the front; others believed they were destined for garrison duties in Egypt, South Africa or India, there to free the regular troops for war service. Yet others openly stated that the war would be over by the time they finished mucking about with all this training nonsense - ***'Give us rifles and let us at the Hun!'*** was the cry oft heard. Still the war went on.

The situation was bleak. The British Expeditionary Force (BEF) had all but been routed at Mons. Then, elements under the able command of General Sir Horace Smith-Dorien had fought the

A group of 5th Green Howards leaving Scarborough railway station in 1914, bound for Darlington.

Germans to a temporary standstill at Le Cateau, thus allowing the main bulk of the beleaguered British regular forces to withdraw without being encircled; something which had been seriously threatened.

The Battle of the Marne had seen the BEF rally and push the enemy back for five consecutive days and nights, while the Battle of the Aisne had seen the Germans hold their ground and the BEF's remarkable advance brought to a shuddering standstill. Then followed the Battles of La Bassée, Messines and Armentières, still with no substantive breakthrough.

The First Battle of Ypres, in Flanders - consisting of several battles at Langemarck, Gheluvelt and Nonne Bosschen - had proved indecisive, yet had left the British seriously weakened and vulnerable against a foe both better prepared and superior in number.

Back in Yorkshire, the devastating news of the decimation of the Regular 2nd Green Howards after their heroic stand at the Menin Cross Roads, during the Battle for Gheluvelt, hit home - hard; from a strength of over 1,000 the Battalion had been reduced to just 300. Every battalion of the Regiment now knew something of what was to face them when they arrived in France.

The onset of a terrible winter, coupled with the reluctance of the German High Command to sanction further large-scale attacks, eventually slowed the frantic pace of those first few months of war, the heavy rain leaving the low-lying Flanders' plains one vast sea of mud. On the Western Front nothing moved, neither side made gains; a stalemate ensued, and with it the misery and blight of the trenches had begun. The war looked set to drag on into the new year, past the Christmas conclusion that many had first forecast.

Suddenly the carnage and blood of war spread from the Western Front to the home front, as the north-east's coastal towns were bombarded from the sea by elements of the German High Seas Fleet.

The folk of Scarborough and Hartlepool awoke, on the 16th December 1914, to the cacophony of war as German warships, hell-bent on destruction, sent a withering barrage of high-explosive shells raining down on the unprotected and the innocent. The towns, especially Scarborough - whose small detachment of Royal Garrison Artillery Territorials had recently been moved from the town, leaving it undefended - were left littered with the mayhem of war, the streets strewn with dead and wounded. In the aftermath of the attacks, as

An artist's impression of the bombardment of Scarborough, 16th December 1914.

Shell damage to houses in Lonsdale Road (left) and St Nicholas Street (right), Scarborough, 16th December 1914, caused by elements of the German High Seas Fleet.

the injured were cared for, the dead buried, and the damage made good, the young men of Scarborough vowed to have their revenge; for the hideous deaths of 19 innocent civilians, among them women, children and a fourteen-month old baby, and for the wounding and maiming of dozens of others.

The loathsome destruction of the east-coast resort only served to stiffen the resolve of the men of the 5th Battalion as they continued preparing for war. How much longer would they have to wait to get at the enemy and settle the score? No one answered, for at that stage no one knew.

The townsfolk, shocked and grieving, demanded the Germans be tried for murder. Hastily prepared and printed recruitment posters screamed at the nation's youth, ***'REMEMBER SCARBOROUGH!'***; and eager volunteers from across the region, flushed with a heady mixture of anger and resentment, flocked to join the colours. The local regiment became the place to be, khaki the colour of the moment, and so great was the influx of recruits that a 'second-line' 5th Battalion was formed; thus the original Battalion was designated 1/5th Green Howards, and the Second-Line Battalion 2/5th Green Howards. The 2/5th would never see active service in their own right, but would provide drafts of replacements for the 1/5th.

Hardly had the dust of the bombardment settled than there came strange tales from the Western Front of Christmas Day truces; of friend and foe exchanging gifts on the frozen, hard-bitten, hard fought for ground of no-man's-land; of carols sung in English and German by sworn enemies; of football matches played in between the trenches; of hearty laughter, jovial back-slapping and good humoured handshakes. Was it true? Had these things really happened? ***And with the barbarous Bosche to boot!***

The war dragged on through the harshness of winter. A new year dawned, and with it the appalling conditions on the Western Front continued. No one doubted now that the war would last long enough for everyone to see some action.

In Britain Field Marshal Lord Kitchener, the Secretary of State for War, began to raise his New Armies, armies filled to overflowing with volunteers, for there was as yet no shortage of men and no conscription. The Pals' battalions were born, and from every town and village, and every workplace and school droves of eager young men enlisted to serve with their mates. But despite their almost unseemly haste to

Shell damage in Wykeham Street.

Damage to the lighthouse Vincent's Pier.

Shell damage to Merryweather's shop, Prospect Road, Scarborough, 16th December 1914: one fatality and several injured.

get to the front it would be almost two full years before these new Kitchener battalions saw active service.

March brought the British offensive against the Aubers Ridge; a strategically important landmark which the Germans held in force, and from where their artillery observers were able to call down thunderous barrages as soon as any member of the BEF so much as sneezed. Yet despite methodical and robust planning the ridge, heavily defended, was never taken; instead the focus and objective of the offensive became the battered village of Neuve Chapelle at its foot.

The BEF enjoyed rare early success, taking the village quickly and consolidating its gain. However, unable to follow through in strength and hampered by supply shortages, the advance petered out and any hoped-for additional gains were lost. During the three-day battle the Germans brought up huge amounts of reinforcements, plugged the gaps in their lines and strengthened their defences. The British could do no more and the offensive slithered into the soul-stealing Flanders' mud.

The stalemate returned with a vengeance; and it was into this that the young men of Yorkshire were about to come, full of life, with their high spirits and eager anticipation, tempered by the recent memory of the fate of their own 2nd Battalion - only recently brought back to strength by a massive influx of five hundred replacements.

In France the Regular Army had held, but at such huge cost that it would never be the same again. The Regular Army had all but ceased to exist and in Britain the New Army battalions, on which Kitchener unreasonably pinned such high hopes, were far from ready. There was no one else to send into the fray. No one else to fill the breach. It was finally time for Britain's *'Saturday Night Soldiers'* to be summoned to battle. Time finally to test their Terrier mettle against the might of the Imperial German Army.

So, at long last, the 5th Green Howards, now considered ready by the British High Command, made their final preparations to join the bruised and battered BEF in France.

Ahead of the Battalion went an 85 strong detachment, led by Captain James Thomson, to organise transportation and to facilitate its smooth and safe passage to the front. The party, including transport and machine-gun officers (there were still only two Maxim machine-guns per Battalion at this point in the war), left Newcastle for Southampton on the 15th April. They sailed for France early the

A view of Northumberland Street, Newcastle, from where the 5th Green Howards went to war.

"Crossing the Channel was quite thrilling. But an old BEF man rather spoiled the whole trip by swanking without his lifebelt, and otherwise showing everybody the entire thing was far from new to him."

next day as the remainder of the Battalion, bristling with weapons and weighed down with equipment and kit, travelled to London by train as the 50th Division moved from the north of England to northern France.

> Saturday 17th April 1915
> *It's been a long time in coming but we're finally on our way to the front. We left Newcastle by train at 11.30 this morning, passing Lincoln, Spalding, March and Cambridge. Despite the early start we didn't arrive at London's Liverpool Street Station until 8.15pm - it was a long and tiring journey. We changed trains and left London at 8.40pm bound for Folkestone. Arrived there at 10.45pm and at once boarded the transport ship 'Onward'.*
> *Sailed at 11.30pm, bound for Boulogne. Too excited to sleep. It's dark, and quiet, and most of us want to be alone with our thoughts - though packed in below decks as we are it's difficult. None of us know what it'll be like once we're there, none of us know what to expect.*
> [Private Jim Stevenson, writing in his diary.]

For many it was their first sea crossing, and for a few their first journey outside their native towns and villages, but all of them held to their own private thoughts and fears. They had said their goodbyes, and, not a few, had made their peace with God. All the preparation and training was over, done with, finished. Now they were bound for the front to face the enemy; there to either prove or embarrass themselves. In their hearts they knew which it would be, come the day they met the Hun.

The Battalion's much admired and respected Commanding Officer, Lieutenant-Colonel Sir Mark Sykes, was fated to stand and watch as his precious 5th Green Howards travelled abroad without him. A severe throat infection forced him to stay in England, and by the time he had recovered sufficiently to take up the reins of command once more the War Office, in its infinite wisdom and much to his chagrin, ordered that he remain behind to advise on matters of 'national and military importance'. For a man so utterly dedicated to

A typical British troop ship -
this one is loading at Southampton.

The first destination for the advance party of
the 5th Green Howards, the harbour and port of Le Havre.
Pictured here well before the war.

the Regiment and his Battalion to be kept at home was bitterly disappointing. Some time later, by way of assuaging that disappointment, he would add brasses and tablets to the Eleanor Cross at Sledmere thus creating a lasting memorial to the Battalion's fallen, a shrine which he earnestly hoped would one day become a place of pilgrimage for those who had served and survived, and for the families of those who had perished.

The Battalion now came under the able command of Major James Mortimer, an experienced soldier who had enlisted in 1880 at the age of 17 in the 2nd Volunteer Battalion The East Yorkshire Regiment. Mortimer had risen through the ranks, serving as a Captain with the Volunteer Active Service Company of that unit during the Boer War. As Sir Mark's trusted second-in-command, and as a much respected officer, it was only right and fitting that he assume command of the Battalion.

The 5th Green Howards landed in France in the early hours of Sunday 18th April 1915. Many of them would never leave, others would return shattered and broken, and only a few would come through unscathed; but between now and then there was a war to be fought.

> Sunday 18th April 1915
> *We've arrived safely in France. Docked at Boulogne at 1.15am, disembarked with kit and marched out of the town, up the hill to St Martin's Camp. Arrived there at 2.30am. It's bitterly cold and we're having a very uncomfortable time of it . . . fifteen men to a tent, and only one blanket each.*
> [Private Jim Stevenson, writing in his diary.]

It was usual for fresh units arriving in France to be given a short period in the trenches under instruction from more seasoned troops. However, this was not to be the case for the 5th Green Howards. At fifteen minutes past midnight on Monday 19th they were hastily assembled with full kit and marched out of St Martin's Camp to form part of V Corps Reserve (Second Army).

The 5th Battalion, together with the 4th Green Howards, the 4th East Yorkshire Regiment, and the 5th Durham Light Infantry formed the 150th (1st York and Durham) Brigade of the 50th (Northumbrian)

The Infantry Battalions of the 50th Northumbrian Division, April 1915

4th and 5th Green Howards

5th, 6th, 7th, 8th and 9th Durham Light Infantry

4th East Yorkshires

5th Border Regiment

4th, 5th, 6th and 7th Northumberland Fusiliers

Division - the first full Territorial division to serve on the Western Front. Between them the four battalions of the 150th Brigade accounted for the recruitment of a great part of north-east England with their Headquarters being located at Scarborough (5th Green Howards), Northallerton (4th Green Howards), Hull (4th East Yorkshires) and Stockton-on-Tees (5th Durhams).

The fact that they were all Terriers and that they hailed from the 'same' part of the world gave them an uncommonly strong bond, a bond which was to stand them in good stead throughout the war as they went in and out of the line together, fought together and often died together.

> Monday 19th April 1915
> *We've had very little rest. We left St Martin's Camp at 12.15am and marched about 5 miles to Pont-de-Briques - some went by cattle-truck. The night is pitch black.*
>
> *At Pont-de-Briques we boarded a train, but did not leave there until 3.15am. Arrived at Cassel, on the Belgian border, at 9.00am. There followed a hot and tiring 12 mile march to our allotted billets in farms outside of Steenvoorde. My billet is in Monte Malise farm - in one of the outbuildings. We're now officially in Corps Reserve.*
>
> *We can hear the guns at the front from here - there's a very heavy bombardment going on.*
> [Private Jim Stevenson, writing in his diary.]

The area about Steenvoorde had been designated as the mustering point for the entire 50th Division, much as Newcastle had been back home. It was here that the 150th Brigade joined with the two other infantry Brigades of the Division, the 149th and the 151st; these Brigades being made up of battalions from the Northumberland Fusiliers and the Durham Light Infantry respectively, with a battalion of the Border Regiment joining first one Brigade and then the other.

The Battalion spent the next three days billeted close to the village of Steenvoorde, well within earshot of the thunderous bombardment at the front - the precursor to what would become known, all too soon, as the **'Second Battle of Ypres'**.

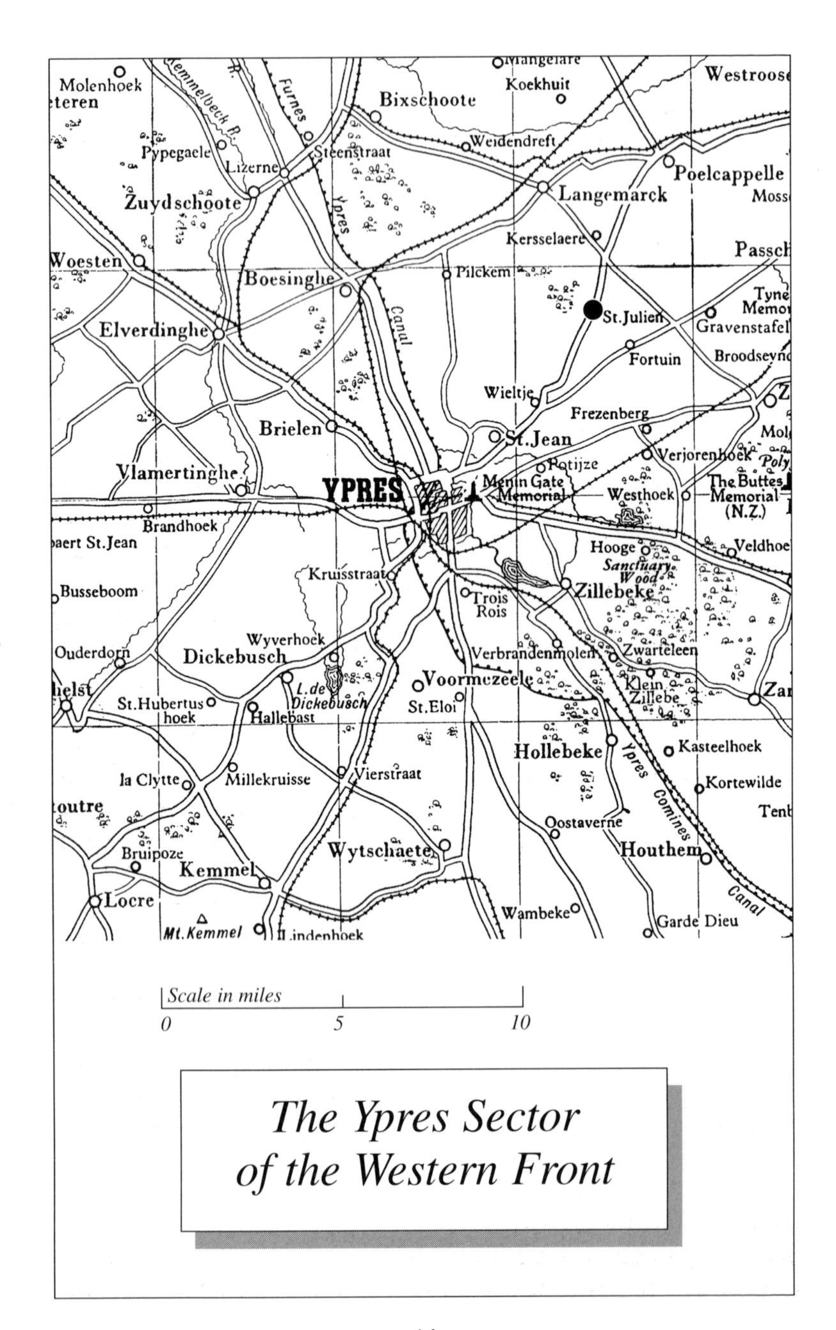

The Ypres Sector of the Western Front

We've been through some fine country while moving up. Along every wayside crosses abound. Most of the farms are now worked by women, old men and boys, the capable men being in the ranks. It's astonishing how hard the women work, and they seem to like it. In most farms hereabouts the Germans have been in and taken the best of everything.

[Corporal Tom Little, writing home.]

Nervous and uncomfortable, the men made their final preparations to enter the line, checking equipment and kit, and attending to any last-minute problems. They were kept busy by their officers, many of them - often no older than the men they led - facing the prospect of their first action too. Parades, route-marches and drills were organised in an attempt to quell their ever-increasing nerves.

The battle, raging close by, was based around the ancient town of Ypres, in what was known as the 'Ypres Salient'; an infamous and dangerous bulge in the Allied line overlooked and fired on from three sides by the enemy.

It was here, during the battle for Gravenstafel Ridge, on the 22nd, that the Germans used poison gas for the first time in their attempt to wrest 'Hill 60' from the Allies. In reality the hill was little more than an overgrown spoil heap, a low ridge 250 yards in length, formed during the excavation of cuttings for the railway and named for the 60 metre spot height marked on the Allied maps - but it was vigorously fought over nonetheless. Any trace of trenches on the 'hill' had long since disappeared and its surface was nothing more than shell craters littered with the debris of war and the bodies of the dead.

Shortly after 5.00pm French, Canadian and British troops were subjected to an horrendous enemy attack using chlorine gas. The advance of the thick, swirling yellow-green vapour towards the Allied trenches caused chaos and mayhem, and exacted heavy casualties among the Allies. The French, with no anti-gas protection of any kind, were forced to withdraw from the front line. By dusk the same day the villages of Langemarck and Pilckem had fallen into enemy hands. The Germans' planned advance was only brought to a halt by a hastily improvised British and Canadian defensive line;

Citizens about to flee another town, while two bemused German soldiers (foreground) look on.

A view of the Yser Canal in the Ypres sector where the 5th Green Howards first dug in.

and by their infantry's reluctance to rush headlong into their own gas.

> *The effect of these poisonous gases was so virulent as to render the whole of the line held by the French divisions practically incapable of any action at all. It was at first impossible for anyone to realise what had actually happened. The smoke and fumes hid everything from sight, and hundreds of men were thrown into a comatose or dying condition, and within an hour the whole position had to be abandoned, together with about fifty guns.*
> [The BEF's Commander-in-Chief, Field Marshal Sir John French writing in his Despatches.]

Though near by when the initial attack took place, the Battalion was not involved. Indeed, the only unit of the 50th Division actively serving on the battle front at the time was Newcastle's 1st Northumbrian Field Ambulance. This unit had been ordered to join elements of the 5th Division at an Advance Dressing Station housed in the old Asylum building at Ypres - one of the few buildings still standing. Having arrived and set to work treating the wounded and injured, they were suddenly alarmed to be confronted by hordes of French troops swarming through the ruins of the place heading straight for the rear.

> *Something has happened! Everybody is very excited. The town is crowded with French Colonial troops, Turcos and others, and reports say they have fled from their posts, having been attacked by some poisonous gas used by the Germans. The bombardment has lessened considerably, but nobody yet knows exactly what has happened.*
> [Colonel H. S. Thurston, The Assistant Director of Medical Services of the 1st Northumbrian Field Ambulance, Territorial Force (TF) writing in his diary.]

British artillery passing through a French town on their way to the front.

The 'unwelcome' German Infantry buying and drinking 'lemonade' from the locals.

With news of the attack filtering through to support and reserve troops alike, the 5th Green Howards weren't in the least surprised when they received orders at midnight to ***'move up, nearer the front'***.

At the time no one seriously thought they would be thrown straight into the fray; no, it was simply that they were moving up as a precautionary measure. The Transport and Machine-Gun Sections followed on shortly afterwards, while behind them they left a handful of men from the Battalion's 'A' Company, under the command of a Quartermaster, as a guard.

> Friday 23rd April 1915
> *This morning we packed up, left our billets and marched into Steenvoorde. Arrived there at 1.30pm and boarded motor buses bound for the front. We were packed in like sardines. Had an uncomfortable ride through Abeele, Poperinghe and Vlamertinghe to a camp at Brielen, just north-west of Ypres. There were hundreds of Belgians on the road fleeing from Ypres, many carrying their worldly goods on their backs or in small carts. Women and children too - a very sorry sight. There were also some of our own lads, much the worse for the gassing and completely out of touch with their units.*
>
> *We slept in huts near to the firing line - though it was hard to sleep properly so close to the front.*
> [Private Jim Stevenson, writing in his diary.]

The Battalion, now placed under the general command of 28th Division, grabbed what rest it could at Brielen as other battalions of its Brigade, the 150th, took up positions along the banks of the Yser Canal, north-west of Ypres at the Brielen bridge - there to support Brigadier-General Wanless O'Gowan's 13th Brigade (part of the 5th Division), if required.

In the wee small hours of Saturday 24th, the entire 150th Brigade was ordered out of billets and told to move up and occupy defensive positions on the canal bank. The 5th Green Howards took their allotted position - minus their precious machine-guns - on the extreme left of the British line, in support of the 2nd Zouave Battalion,

The ruined railway station at Ypres,
ever a familiar sight to the British Tommy.

A typical ruined village,
the remains of Bailleul in the Ypres sector.

Colonial troops of the French Army, and settled down to wait. After all their preparation and training they were finally about to make their entrance into the greatest conflict the world had ever seen.

> Saturday 24th April 1915
> *Up at 2.15am and marched to the trenches in silence and pitch darkness. Verey lights [signal flares] are bursting overhead and the flash of guns lights up the sky. Passed a dressing station - it was very busy with many casualties. Arrived at the front at 4.20am. We're in some trenches with Algerian Zouaves of the French Army - they gave us a breakfast of red wine, bread and sardines. We had a number of casualties from the shellfire while moving up. Miserable conditions at night, heavy rain all night.*
> [Private Jim Stevenson, writing in his diary.]
>
> *The Algerian troops have been very good to our men, sharing their food when ours was scarce.*
> [Company Sergeant Major Thompson, writing home.]

The withdrawal of the French from the Allied line allowed large numbers of German infantry to cross the Yser Canal, near the village of Steenstraate, and then to dig themselves in. The 5th Battalion thus found itself with the enemy front line just three hundred yards north-east of its position, and though still technically 'in support' there were no other friendly troops between it and the enemy.

As dawn of the 24th broke over Flanders and the early morning mist cleared, the Yorkshiremen got their first proper view of the infamous Ypres Salient. The ancient city, home to Belgian cloth-workers, was to their right flank and still resembled something of its former self - its ruins not readily apparent from this distance. Around and about them the whole of their Battalion area was scarred, blistered and battered by the continuous shelling from both sides' artillery.

It was a disquieting scene and men already nervous bit down on their lips and swallowed hard at the rising bile. This was what they

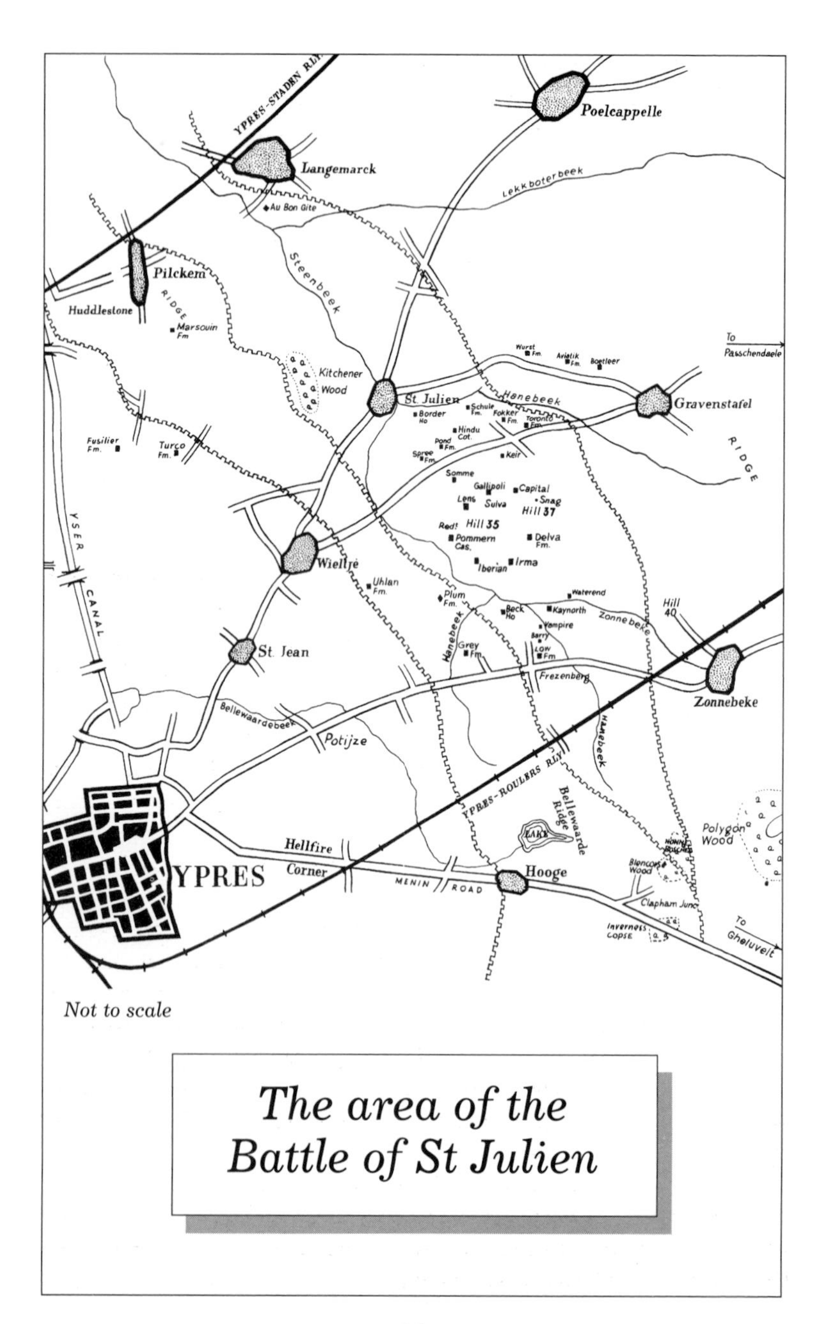

The area of the Battle of St Julien

had volunteered for, this was what they had trained so long for, very soon they would be called upon and hoped they would not be found wanting in anyone's eyes, least of all those of their own comrades.

The early hours of the morning passed slowly and quietly, until precisely 10.00am when the Germans opened with a terrific bombardment against the entrenched British positions. Fortunately the enemy artillery's range was somewhat long and the majority of their shells fell behind the 5th Battalion's lines. The barrage continued throughout the remainder of the morning and despite its ferocious intensity only two men from 'B' Company were injured.

At midday the Battalion, along with an attached machine-gun section from the 7th Northumberland Fusiliers under the command of Second-Lieutenant Craig, was ordered to Potijze, a march of several hours, ***'there to place itself at the disposal of any Brigadier requiring assistance'.***

Crossing the canal by way of a rickety pontoon bridge the men moved hurriedly towards Potijze. As they passed St Jean, on their left, they witnessed Canadian units being forced out of the blazing town by the enemy. Under orders which strictly prevented them from lending assistance, the 5th Battalion pressed on in *'skirmish formation'*. Immediately on their arrival at Potijze, in mid-afternoon, the 5th Green Howards were sent to assist Brigadier-General Turner's 3rd (Canadian) Infantry Brigade at nearby St Julien where, they were told, the Germans had attacked with poison gas and broken through.

Tired and weary, weighed down by their enormous packs, the men trudged on.

Arriving outside gas-laden St Julien the Battalion found the plucky Canadians, using handkerchiefs, towels and bandages soaked in water and urine as improvised gas masks, had managed to stand their ground and contain the German advance inside the town. Indeed a major counter-attack was already being organised by Brigadier-General Hull, 10th Brigade (4th Division), and the 5th Green Howards were ordered to take up supporting positions left of the British line in front of St Julien.

The counter-attack, bravely led and carried out with great grit and determination, nevertheless failed. The Germans remained in control of the battered town. The losses sustained by Brigadier-General Hull's 10th Brigade alone during the attack amounted to some

*This was once the main road through a village;
now only a single barn is left standing.*

*At the start of the war many French roads were tree-lined,
however, within months barely any remained unscathed.*

73 officers and 2,346 other ranks out of its four battalions' combined strength of over 4,000.

Unable to make contact with and obtain orders from their own 150th Brigade Headquarters, the 5th Green Howards were placed under the command of a Canadian General who readily employed them to reinforce his precarious trench lines.

> Order to the Commanding Officer
> 5th Battalion, Green Howards:
> *You will take up a position and entrench in rear of our present line in C.16.C. [a map reference] You will be ready to counter-attack when necessary.*
> Lieutenant-Colonel G. B. Hughes
> 3rd Canadian Infantry Brigade.
> Saturday 24th April 1915

The British and weakened Canadians dug in and waited. As the evening progressed the enemy, seeing a possible advantage, pressed forward bent on breaking the joint Canadian and British line. Fighting hard alongside the Canadian units the 5th Green Howards repelled the enemy and stubbornly held onto their positions until the early hours of the following morning; their net losses for the night being one man killed and several others wounded.

At 3.00am, on the 25th, after a harrowing night spent under both bombardment and heavy rain, the Battalion was ordered to retire and make room in the trenches for relieving battalions from the Seaforth Highlanders and the Royal Irish Rifles. While the Canadians moved back for a rest, the Green Howards were ordered to proceed to nearby Fortuin, there to offer assistance to any unit requiring it. Along the way to their new position the Battalion passed large numbers of men, detached from their various units, and in retreat.

Two hours later the Battalion arrived at its designated rendezvous point along with the 5th Durham Light Infantry. Here the General Officer Commanding the 150th Brigade, Brigadier-General Bush, met with his senior officers to discuss the situation and conditions of the various units and to issue fresh orders.

Out of the trenches, wet, cold and uncomfortable, the men of the 5th Green Howards finally marched back the way they had come, to a

King George V visiting the gallant Canadian troops.

'Three English Heroes'
A French artist's view of the brave British artillerymen.

field close to the Zaaerebeke stream, on the road to Wieltje, there, still within earshot of the battle, to rest awhile and await developments.

Less than an hour later, just after 6.00am, the Battalion was hurriedly gathered and moved forward again to support the Seaforths and the Irish who were now falling back from an enemy gas attack. As it advanced on St Julien, across open fields, the 5th Battalion met with very heavy high-explosive artillery fire and suffered appallingly, with some sixty casualties in just five minutes. Among the wounded was the Battalion's Adjutant, Captain Stuart Grant-Dalton; an experienced soldier who had been with the Regiment since 1906, and who had earned himself quite a reputation as a sharpshooter. Now, in this, his first serious encounter with the enemy, he had been badly mauled and was to be sent home, taking no further part in the fortunes of the 5th Green Howards. Second-Lieutenant Majolier now took up the duties and responsibilities of the Battalion Adjutant, the Commanding Officer's Staff Officer.

Eventually, unable to continue forward under the hail of fire from the enemy, the Battalion was pulled back and deployed, taking up positions on a line facing St Julien and Fortuin; 'B' and 'C' Companies were formed up in the trenches, while 'A' and 'D' Companies were in the bottom of a hedgerow which lined the left-hand side of the road, along with the attached machine-gun section from the 7th Northumberlands. Situated in trenches on the 5th Battalion's right flank were the 5th Durhams.

The enemy, exploiting the breach made by their gas, advanced in force and the Battalion was forced to maintain a rapid rate of rifle fire just to slow their pace. Then, at 10.00am sharp the German infantry suddenly halted, threw themselves down on the ground and began digging in at a furious pace. The Green Howards, correctly fearing the worst, scrambled to find what cover they could, digging with their entrenching tools and hands as a withering enemy bombardment was launched against them.

Pinned down by shell and determined enemy machine-gun fire from a nearby farmhouse, the Battalion's casualty rate continued to rise. By noon the situation was precarious, to say the least, and in order to try and relieve some of the pressure Captain Geoffrey Barber, Commanding 'D' Company, was ordered to occupy the farmhouse ahead of them. To do this not only would he have to silence the

British observation balloon (of the 'sausage' variety) about to take to the Flanders' skies.

A ruined village (the remains of the church are in the right foreground) deep within the devastated Ypres sector.

machine-gun hidden there, but also take the farmhouse and then hold it against the enemy; it was an almost impossible task. However, undaunted by the challenge facing him, Captain Barber selected a twenty-five strong group of men from 'D' Company, took Lieutenant Harold Brown as his second-in-command and Lance-Corporal Claude Dell as his NCO, and set off to get the job done.

Leading his men, revolver in hand, Captain Barber moved forward under covering fire from his own lines. Despite the appalling conditions of flying bullets and shells the party somehow managed to gain ground close to the farmhouse and successfully knocked out the machine-gun. Almost at once they were met with heavy shell and machine-gun fire from all sides; the enemy having had the building in their sights throughout. The party, caught in the open was enfiladed by machine-guns and Captain Barber was killed, as were Lance-Corporal Dell and nine men. The remains of the party, now under the command of Lieutenant Brown, unable to achieve the objective or hold onto their position, could do nothing but fall back under the intense enemy fire.

The Battalion's defensive line was now ordered to be held ***'at all cost'***, there being no 'support' or 'secondary line' upon which it might fall back; in effect the Battalion was the only remaining barrier to a German advance. However, with small enemy units spotted moving up to occupy trenches north of the Battalion's position, runners were sent off to Brigade HQ with the message, ***'Enemy inclined to press. Have you any orders?'*** No reply was returned. Whether this was due to there being no orders, or, as is more likely the case, the runners becoming casualties and failing to return to the Battalion during the action, remains unclear.

The enemy barrage that had begun at 10.00am continued non-stop throughout the day until 5.00pm, when, mercifully, it eased somewhat. From then on, and through the night, the Battalion was treated to intermittent bursts of shell and machine-gun fire, forcing them to keep their heads down. The Battalion's last recorded fatality of the day was Sergeant David Joy, killed in the act of supervising his men.

That night, over ground lit by flashes of occasional shellfire, the 5th Green Howards cautiously moved out from their trenches to recover their dead and wounded; to be buried, or evacuated to the nearest Advance Dressing Station. Lieutenant Brown, who had led 'D' Company's badly mauled party back from the farmhouse earlier

'There goes our blinkin' parapet again!'
by Captain Bruce Bairnsfather, who was, without doubt,
the soldiers' favourite war artist. Bairnsfather's 'Old Bill'
became synonymous with the beleaguered and hard-pressed Tommy.
As a Lieutenant with the Warwickshire Regiment he arrived in
France just after the Battle of Mons and was serving in the
Ypres sector in April 1915, during the Second Battle of Ypres.

in the day, now went out himself to gather in the body of Lance-Corporal Dell; this done he then personally oversaw the burial of the NCO. This act was noted by the men and earned Lieutenant Brown much quiet admiration and respect; which was later to stand him in good stead when he called for volunteers to carry out a particularly hazardous raid.

The following day, the 26th, some slight relief from the heavy shelling and near constant sniping of the Battalion's position was obtained when the 149th Brigade and the Lahore Division advanced on St Julien, thus drawing off the enemy fire. These attackers succeeded in entering and holding the southernmost portion of the town for a short time, before being driven back to a line on the left of the 5th Green Howards' trenches and to the south of the town. During the day, the farmhouse which had been the objective of Captain Barber's ill-fated raid, received a direct hit by a German incendiary shell and was totally destroyed.

> Monday 26th April 1915
> *Dawn - another thick mist all round. Stuck in trenches all day - 'A' Company suffered many casualties from the shelling and continuous sniping. Left the trenches at 8.30pm for the second time to dig more trenches - it was a quiet night, except for occasional shellfire. We later moved forward with the 5th Durhams to relieve the London Regiment.*
> [Private Jim Stevenson, writing in his diary.]

The 5th Green Howards hung on grimly throughout the rest of the day. With no immediate relief in sight they were forced to spend another uncomfortable night in the trenches, continually subjected to enemy shelling and sniping. At 8.30pm they were ordered forward to take over a line of trenches, in what was called the Horseshoe, from the London Regiment. Here again they suffered a number of casualties. During the night and early hours of the morning they did what they could to improve the trenches.

By the following day, the 27th, a fresh Allied line had been formed slightly north of them and a battalion of the Royal Fusiliers had taken up residence there. The day was spent warily repairing and

British officers in a makeshift reserve camp, where an officer is in conversation with a French liaison officer (to the right of the picture).

More destruction and ruin in the Ypres sector, this time at the village of Locre.

improving the trenches, rifles always to hand in case of enemy action. Despite being no longer in direct sight of St Julien, the 5th Green Howards still proved to be well within range of the enemy guns and were continuously shelled throughout the day. The width and shallowness of their trenches meant that they suffered more from the shelling than would otherwise have been the case had they been well entrenched, and because of this their casualties rose steadily. There was nothing they could do about it. Unable to work on the trenches in daylight for fear of being shelled or sniped at, they were forced to spend what little time they could at night making good the damage inflicted during the day.

Towards evening a battalion of the London Regiment moved forward to take up positions three-quarters of a mile to the north-east of the Green Howards' trenches, strengthening the British line against a possible German attack - all too frequently presaged by the type of barrage they had been subjected to all day. The Germans however, apparently happy where they were, able to shell and shoot at will anything that moved, made no effort to advance.

> Tuesday 27th April 1915
> *Still in forward trenches - at Horseshoe. The Royal Fusiliers and the London Regiment are with us. Much shelling. A German shell destroyed our rations and water so we had to go without. Improved the trenches at night - much digging. All are hungry and thirsty - drank from puddles at the bottom of the trench. The water is foul and dirty but there is no other to be had.*
> [Private Jim Stevenson, writing in his diary.]

The enemy's artillery not only destroyed what few provisions the Battalion had in its trenches, but also prevented any supplies from being brought up from the rear. The men were forced to go without and live on whatever tinned rations they had, and such water as could be found around them.

Overhead, meanwhile, flights of enemy aircraft droned, ranging for their gunners and then swooping low to drop bombs on the unfortunate men below. Only the night, with its sheltering darkness, brought them some small respite.

*A typical Advanced Field Ambulance station,
with ambulances ready to shuttle the wounded back to base.*

Yet more ruins in the infamous Ypres sector.

In the following days they were subjected to more of the same, the men constantly forced to try and dodge the shellfire in order to carry out what duties they could. It was a hellish time, cramped into funkholes and muddy trenches with no food, no water, and precious little peace; and all the time the threat of a massive German attack hung over them.

Late in the evening of 29th April the 5th Green Howards, under the welcome cover of darkness, were relieved by the men of their own 4th Battalion and the 4th East Yorkshires (both units of the 150th Brigade).

> *Made our way there through that hell on earth by now strewn with dead animals and bits of everything recognisable in the way of equipment, through St Jean, now utterly destroyed and slightly more objectionable than even Ypres; church gutted, graveyard shelled and a heap of coffins and battered headstones.*
>
> *The 10th Brigade (of the 4th Division) to which we were attached, had headquarters here - a cottage sand-bagged round - and the shots from a battery of ours just touched the tops of the trees as we passed.*
>
> *We found our supply dump and by and by the trenches. Sorry trenches they were, freshly made, very bad, narrow, with scarcely any traverses, nothing at all behind and only funkholes for shelter.*
>
> [Captain B. M. R. Sharp, 4th East Yorkshires, writing in his diary.]

The men of the 5th Green Howards left the trenches at 11.15pm and marched wearily back to their former camp at Brielen. They arrived at the huts, tired and exhausted, at 2.00am in the early hours of 30th April.

However, no sooner had they taken up residence again than they were shelled by the enemy's long-range guns and forced to quit the relative comfort of the huts and dig shelter trenches for themselves near by.

The BEF's C-in-C, Sir John French, replaced by his deputy, Haig, in December 1915, returned to England to become C-in-C of the home forces. He was one of the few officers of the High Command who believed in the worthiness of the untried Terriers - a belief borne out by the events of April 1915.

We're just about getting used to the shells and shrapnel now. I'm writing in a field near a rest camp. A shell has burst 200 yards behind me, a piece hitting a chap, almost severing his arm off. [Private Frank Ware, writing home.]

Later in the day the shelling eased a little and the men were allowed to return to the huts to rest properly. Here Captain Crockatt took over the duties and responsibilities of the Battalion Adjutant from Second-Lieutenant Majolier and began the tasks of bringing the Battalion's Diary up to date and of recording the names of the dead and wounded.

As night fell, so too did the shells. The 5th Green Howards were rudely forced from their huts and into their funkholes once more by a shower of '*Jack Johnsons*' - the German 150mm heavy howitzer shells, renowned for their loud noise and black smoke explosions, and nick-named after the black, heavyweight boxing champion of 1909 to 1915.

The round of shelling and vacating the huts continued for the next couple of days, when suddenly news of another enemy gas attack began coming in. Hard on its heels followed hundreds of gassed men, threading their way through the camp as they were led to the rear. It was a thoroughly sickening sight and some small alarm was raised by the belief that the Germans were about to attack in force.

Acting on the assumption that the Germans would indeed follow the gas with an infantry assault, the 5th Green Howards were summarily mustered, marched from the camp and out onto the Poperinghe-Ypres road, where they took up positions to lie in wait for whatever might turn up.

Nothing did, and the Battalion, much to its relief, was marched off; this time away from Brielen, by way of Brandhoek and Abeele to huts nearer Ypres.

The Battalion's first action in the war had effectively ended.

It was with a sense of needing a well-earned rest that the Green Howards spent the day in bivouacs near Vlamertinghe on 2nd May, before marching on again at 9.15pm bound for Steenvoorde. Finally, on 3rd May, camped just outside the village of Steenvoorde, the Battalion was able to rest properly for the first time since landing in France.

General Herbert Plumer, Commander of the 2nd Army Corps at the time of the Second Battle of Ypres, was considered one of the most able and popular of the British commanders.

During the days of Second Ypres, in their first fully-fledged action of the Great War, the 5th Green Howards had lost one officer and twenty-three men killed, and had one officer and one hundred and six non-commissioned officers and men wounded, of whom six were later to die of their wounds; this from a strength of just over 1,000.

The following day, Tuesday 4th May, to their surprise they were paraded on the roadside to be formally inspected and addressed by the Commander-in-Chief of the British Expeditionary Force, Field Marshal Sir John French.

> *I have come this morning to express to every single officer and man how much I admire the splendid behaviour of the Battalion in the fighting which has gone on during the last ten days. The 5th Yorkshire Regiment has suffered heavily. You have had one officer killed, one officer wounded, twenty-eight men killed and one hundred and five men wounded.*
>
> *When you came out here you were called upon very hurriedly and you had very little preparation. Things do come that way - very suddenly - in war. The call came through of the disgraceful conduct of the people who are fighting us, who call themselves soldiers, but who behave in a very unsoldierlike way. In the circumstances we could not wait and had to do the best we could. I do not want to go into the details of that fight, because there were other British soldiers engaged. I want particularly to talk of the splendid conduct of the men of the 50th Northumbrian Division, and especially of your Battalion. I wish to compliment every one of you, and I am very grateful to you for all you have done. I think your conduct magnificent.*
>
> *Whenever I am speaking of Territorial soldiers I find it very difficult adequately to express how strongly I feel on the subject. I had a good deal to do with Territorial soldiers before the war, when I was Inspector-General of the Forces, and I have*

The typical burial of a British officer on the Western Front, carried out when it was 'quiet'.

One of the hundreds of temporary cemeteries on the Western Front. This one was in the grounds of a large house at Boesinghe.

always said that when the Territorial Force was called upon, and put to the test, it would not be found wanting.

A good many of our countrymen did not agree with me. But you have shown right well that not only were you found not wanting, but that you were capable of taking your place and fighting splendidly in accordance with the best traditions of the British Army. Your conduct has been superb. Nothing is more difficult than to come out in the ordinary way of routine as you did, and then suddenly to be called upon to fill a breach that has so suddenly been occasioned.

You showed a spirit of splendid patriotism months ago when, leaving your work and homes, you volunteered for foreign service, though originally you had only taken the responsibilities of home defence. This you did in defence of the British Empire, and whilst others remained behind, you have come here to do your duty and have done it and have set a magnificent example.

I am sure that when your fellow-countrymen fully realise your magnificent behaviour, they will thank you as I thank you now. I feel confident that you will keep up the splendid record that you have established whenever you are called upon.

[Sir John French, addressing the 5th Green Howards on the Steenvoorde to Poperinghe road, 4 May 1915.]

It was with a sense of great pride that the Yorkshiremen, already nicknamed the ***'Yorkshire Gurkhas'*** by the 1st Battalion The Princess Victoria's (Royal Irish Rifles) because of their ferocity in attacking the enemy, were dismissed to return to their duties, or billets.

Later the same day, having already earned words of praise from the Canadians and their own Commander-in-Chief, they were paraded again, this time to hear a message from General Plumer, passed on to them by their Battalion Commander.

'As you are supposed to be resting in a quiet spot, a little light literature goes down well!'

A 'quiet' spot in the Ypres sector, where incoming shells were as common as the flies.

In a rare private moment Major Mortimer himself wrote to his wife to tell her of his immense pride in the men he had led into battle; for him there were no finer troops serving anywhere on the Western Front.

> *The Battalion has done splendidly. We were five days in the trenches and the men have stood it well, and with great credit - such trials as no Territorials have experienced as far as I know. All the time, five days, was spent under heavy artillery and rifle fire without a break. The Battalion was shelled very badly, but the men and officers behaved very well. We are all now at a well-earned rest.*
> [Major James Mortimer, Commanding Officer 5th Green Howards.]

The short rest period now afforded the Battalion, and other units of the 50th Division, continued, as did the congratulations and praise on their stout performance, with letters and comments flooding the local and national newspapers from war correspondents and both men and officers of the various units.

> *I'm writing from a rest camp after two days of sheer hell. On Saturday morning we had to get up and form a line on the canal - four casualties then, I think.*
>
> *In the afternoon, the 5th Green Howards and ours made a counter-attack on the Germans, helping the Canadians. After the action we collected up and got home at 2.00am on Sunday. I slept in a cow shed with crowds of others.*
>
> *At 9.00pm we were ordered to some trenches. As we neared them, at some cross-roads, something exploded and I got a very slight bang on the head with a piece of shell. We had a fearful bombardment in those trenches and at 10.00pm we were ordered to others. On arriving there, dog-tired, at 11.00pm, we were then ordered to this*

The Officers of the 1/5th Battalion Alexandra, Princess of Wales's Own Yorkshire Regiment (TF) (The Green Howards)

France, 18th April 1915

Commanding Officer: Major J. Mortimer

Captain & Adjutant: S. Grant-Dalton

Captains:
E. G. C. Bagshawe - G. C. Barber - C. H. Pearce
A. Perl (Royal Army Medical Corps - attached)
J. B. Purvis - F. W. Robson - G. J. Scott - J. A. R. Thomson

Lieutenant & Quartermaster: R. Rennison

Lieutenants:
H. Brown - T. E. Dufty - F. Green - G. A. Maxwell
E. R. Spofforth - J. S. Wadsworth - F. Woodcock

Second-Lieutenants:
F. H. H. Barber - A. F. Clarke - H. S. Cranswick - F. J. Dymond
H. E. Gorst - E. Majolier - G. B. Purvis - E. M. Thompson
G. Thomson - D. P. Tonks - W. Vause

Chaplain: Reverend B. Wolferstan

rest camp, where we arrived at 2.00am today. We're taking things easy now and counting up the cost; the total, in just two days, is 104 casualties.

I expect we shall stay here a day or two then go back to the trenches. The German guns are horrible and the stench from their stink shells makes you weep and cough.

I had a marvellous escape when a machine-gun swept over me, but I got in a hole. The men attacked as if on parade. It was wonderful. They joked too. Shells sent over our heads to a certain city [Ypres] were called 'Main line' and no one ducked. But when we heard them coming to us it was 'Heads Down'.

It is now 3.30pm and I've just had the GOC Northumbrian Division [Major-General Lindsay] here to congratulate me on behalf of the men for the splendid work done by them in stopping the German advance. General Plumer also sent a message after breakfast today.

Our rest camp is like Dante's inferno all night and all day, but I sleep through it all now. Tell the children I saw a spy brought in today. I don't know what shall be done with him - the usual I expect.

Although I have only been here, I suppose, for ten days it seems like 10 years. I've not even seen a German. It is chicken for dinner tonight after four days of bully beef and biscuits.

[Major Arthur Euston, 4th East Yorks, writing home.]

Around them continued Second Ypres, with the battles for Frezenberg Ridge, Bellewaarde Ridge, Aubers Ridge and Festubert. The 5th Green Howards would continue in action well into the year, but for now their first battle was at an end. In the last few days they had not only proved their worth to their many detractors, but had also given the enemy as good as they got.

From here the 5th Green Howards, with their colleagues in the 50th (Northumbrian) Division, went on to play their part in every major

The officers of the 5th Green Howards in 1914 - back row, third from left Robson, fourth Purvis - seated, left to right, Dufty, Mortimer, Sir Mark Sykes (centre), Wetwan (with cane) and Pearce.

battle on the Western Front. They, like many others, would lose heavily on the Somme, at Arras, Passchendaele, the Lys and during the great German offensive of 1918, and precious few of the original Battalion would survive to see the Armistice. As Territorials they had carried a heavy burden to the battlefield, yet in those few short days at the Battle of St Julien they earned the praise and admiration of regular troops of all nations, not least the enemy themselves.

More importantly they had earned the respect of the Army 'establishment' which until then had been so woefully lacking. They had also earned their Regiment's first Territorial Battle Honour of the Great War; it was to be but the first of many.

From their humble beginnings, Territorial volunteers all, raised from the east-coast towns of Scarborough, Bridlington and Whitby, the farming areas of Malton, Pickering, Beverley and Driffield, and all over the north of England, they went on to stoutly and courageously uphold the traditions of a fiercely proud Regiment; Alexandra Princess of Wales's Own Yorkshire Regiment, ***the Green Howards***.

Some forty months after landing in France, just days before the Armistice, the decimated remnants of the 5th Green Howards were sent to other units and the Battalion was officially reduced to Cadre establishment; a tiny nucleus around which a full strength battalion would, perhaps, once more be raised. It was a particularly sad day for those who had got through intact, a day which saw the end of an era, a short but proud era, for they had left their mark; the 5th Green Howards, the ***'Yorkshire Gurkhas'***, would never be forgotten.

The 5th Green Howards at Hummersknott Park in Darlington 1914-15.

The 5th Battalion Green Howards
'In their own write'

The following extracts from letters and verse were written largely by the Scarborough men of the 5th Green Howards. Printed in the local paper at the time, they were read avidly by a local populace eager for news of their lads at the front.

Now, for the first time in over 80 years they again describe, in their own words - intended for families and friends back home - the fateful events of those first few days in France, the days the ***'Yorkshire Gurkhas'*** underwent their ***'Baptism of Fire'***.

It should be noted that where I have stated that a man is not listed as died this only refers to the roll of the battalion he was serving with at the time this narrative describes.

It was often the case, more frequently so towards the end of the war, that men from one battalion, or regiment, found themselves posted to another to make up numbers after heavy losses. In several instances some battalions were disbanded altogether and their personnel distributed far and wide.

Details of the Scarborough and Divisional War Memorials, and the Scarborough Branch of the Old Comrades Association are given in the Epilogue.

With regard to certain references made in the following text to possible errors in the *'Casualty Listing'* for the 5th Battalion, I have taken to highlight any discrepancies for the sole benefit of the reader and for no other reason.

For clarity, the letter or verse always precedes the personal details of those writing or mentioned in the text.

A soldier's service number (where known) always precedes his name and details.

Home addresses are in Scarborough unless otherwise stated.

A group of 5th Green Howards at Hummersknott Park, Darlington in 1914: Private Albert Edward Monkman (seated second right), Private Albert Lincoln (standing third left). The boy with the bayonet is a Boy Scout, attached to the Battalion to run errands.

A group of 5th Green Howards leaving Scarborough railway station in 1914, bound for Darlington.

When we reached France we started travelling about till we got near the firing line. When we got there it was about 8.00pm, and in the morning at 1.30am we were ordered to the trenches.

I was hit by a piece of shrapnel from one of the shells exploding right and left of us. I was in a ditch, filled with water with my head down, when we got the order to get ready to advance. I'd just raised my head when the shell burst and I nearly thought I was a gonner!

Well I was sorry to leave my pals. I've been in about six hospitals. The place was Ypres where I was hit. It's that place where the Germans were trying to break through. I expect to be home before going back again.

Private Whitehead was writing home from the Red Cross Hospital in Sidcup, Kent, after being brought back from the front wounded at the Battle of St Julien. He is not listed as died.

We've had a rough five days in the trenches and are now out for a rest.

War is terrible - dead horses, broken carts, and wounded men lying about everywhere. Alas, the worst sight is the poor refugees, with their bundles, trudging along the roads.

The country hereabouts is in a terrible state, all the roads being like ploughed fields. All the farms are practically destroyed and at night the sky is lit up by burning buildings.

At some of the farms the cattle have been left and you can see the poor things standing looking at their broken-down sheds.

The German artillery is very heavy and they fire constantly. We of 'D' Company were in two very tight corners, but I was fortunate to come out without a scratch.

You have to be careful what you drink hereabouts because the water may be off. We've had a

Sergeants of the 5th Battalion Back row, left to right: J. Moorhouse, J. Hill, W. H. Wilson, P. Foord and D. P. Tonks

Front row, left to right: H. Brooksbank, H. Hugill, P. O. W. Edeson and H. Bradley

lot of German aeroplanes over us, and although fired upon by our lads I saw none brought down. I've lost a lot of weight marching about in the sun!

240975 Private George Frederick Stabler enlisted at Scarborough in January 1915. This letter was written to his parents at 75 Trafalgar Square. George survived until the 17th September 1916, when he died on the Somme. He is commemorated on the Thiepval Memorial, Somme, France, and on the Scarborough War Memorial.

THE GALLANT FIFTH GREEN HOWARDS

It's Saturday morn at Newcastle,
April seventeenth is the date,
And there's a bustle around the station,
The Fifth Green Howards are going to meet fate.

~

There's a true Yorkshire lot going to action,
Against Kaiser and German Huns;
They're off to battle for Britain,
In front of Von Krupp's guns.

~

They're not afraid of the steel, lads,
And the band plays a glorious air;
They're off, and what an ovation,
Is given to those who are doing their share.

~

Now it's Sunday, and two in the morning,
No longer in England they stand,
But on France's fair soil they are stepping,
As brave as any in the land.

~

Just a week since they left dear old England,
And the battle is raging all round,
The Green Howards are holding the centre,
Whilst shells are rending the ground.

~

2/5th Green Howards prior to leaving for France in 1915. George Lightfoot Currey is standing third from left and Private Charles Armstrong is behind him.

The Major says, 'Come on Green Howards!
We are wanted at once at the front;
We are not going back, boys, either,
But will bear the battle's hard brunt.

~

Eagerly they move their position,
And take up a line on their left;
The Royal Irish are fighting on one side,
While Canadians draw blood on the left.

~

These three fine regiments fighting,
Had stemmed a great German advance,
And the Green Howards' first time in action,
Had brought them great fame there in France.

~

Many poor chaps there went under,
But the glory they won will not fade;
They had saved a great situation,
And opened a glorious page.

~

They were once called 'fireside shirkers',
But when England their services needed,
They win a name which is 'Yorkshire Gurkhas',
And for their dear old country they bleed.

~

Twice since have they been in action,
And wrought some glorious deeds;
But the one which was fought at St Julien,
Was where they proved more than weeds.

~

England has known all about them,
And heard, too, of their fame,
Which the Green Howards, as they term them,
Made on the Continent's blood-splattered plain.

~

Then off with your hats to the Green Howards,
A great service they've rendered the land,
They have fought and bled for their country,
And proved they are of real British brand.

2004 Drummer
Harry Betts.

Private
William Betts.

240975 Private
George F. Stabler.

Private
George Betts.

They are only lads at the most now,
But their hearts are in the right spot;
They are as full of grit as they can be,
And for fighting can do quite a lot.

~

So, when the fighting is over,
To England they'll come with the rest,
And be classed at last with the bravest,
The loyalist, truest and best.

~

In history they will be mentioned,
Adding to England's great name,
And for ever their names will be written,
On the glorious scroll of fame.

This poem was found on the body of 1499 Private James Brough, aged 28, by Lance-Corporal George Lightfoot Currey. It was hand-written and is credited to him. James was born in Pickering and enlisted at Malton. He survived until killed in action on the 26th July 1915, while in the Hooge sector. He is buried at the Strand Military Cemetery, Ploegsteert [given the name *'Plug Street'* by the Tommies], Belgium.

Lance-Corporal George Lightfoot Currey, from Scarborough, was a stretcher-bearer with 'D' Company. He is not listed as died.

> *Just a few lines to let you know that I'm all right. I suppose by the time you get this letter the sad news of my poor brother's death will have reached you. I am glad to say that his death was instantaneous and he suffered no pain. I was close by at the time.*
>
> *At present we are relieved from our position in the firing line, and I expect we shall have a rest for a few days now.*
>
> *Do not fret about Harry; he died like a man and a soldier, doing just what was right for any dutiful son towards his parents, relations and friends. To that end has his sacrifice been made. That he may be rewarded for his actions in the next world*

A group of 5th Green Howards in Hummersknott Park Camp, at Darlington in 1914.

is the earnest wish of his brothers and others out here. We are giving the Germans something to go on with. I wish the brutes were all wiped off the face of the earth.

Private William Betts was writing home to his mother at 3 Regent Street, about the death of his brother. He is not listed as died.

2004 Drummer 'Harry' Harold Betts was born in Scarborough. He lived at 60 Tindall Street, and was married with four children. Before the war he was a tailor in a shop on Huntriss Row. Harry enlisted at Scarborough and was wounded at the Battle of St Julien. He later died of his wounds on the 1st May 1915, aged thirty-two. Harry is buried at the Boulogne Eastern Cemetery, Pas de Calais, France, and is commemorated on the Scarborough War Memorial.

There were five Betts brothers serving in the forces, three with the Green Howards and two with the West Yorkshires. However, there are three Betts commemorated on the Scarborough War Memorial, one of whom is Drummer Harry.

The second is his brother, 10375 Ross W. Betts who served with the 18th West Yorkshires, was born in Scarborough and enlisted there. He died on the 27th July 1916, while on the Somme.

The third is believed to be Private George Betts, of the 5th Green Howards, though he is not listed among the Battalion's dead.

SOMEWHERE IN BELGIUM

Out in sunny Belgium,
Are the 5th Green Howards regiment.
We are not out here for pleasure,
but on grim duty bent.
We've been in some fierce fighting,
And earned undying fame,
And hope to do a little more,
To uphold old England's name.

~

We left the old folks at home,
Just for our country's sake.
It matters not how hard our work,
For complaints we never make.

Back, from left to right: Private Thomas J. Mainprize, Miss McNaught and Private Charles Linn. Front: two Canadians and Private H. Waller. Taken at the Auxiliary Military Hospital, Breeze Hill, Bootle, Liverpool.

But there are hundreds now in England,
Who do not care to roam,
To give a helping hand,
To save their loved ones and their home.

~

Before this war commenced,
There were lots of rude comments,
About the poor
Old Terrier Regiments.
But now they've done their bit,
And showed their pluck and grit,
Perhaps they'll get the praise,
Well, just a little bit.

~

When the war is over,
And we return again,
We hope what we've done,
Will not have been in vain.
So here's good luck to the good old Fifth,
Who're sure to make their name,
And perhaps old friends both far and near,
Will wish the lads the same.

Private W. Stonehouse was writing of his pride in his pals and the Battalion. He is not listed as died.

> *No doubt you'd be very much surprised to receive a card to say that I'd been wounded. Well, you've no need to worry, as it's only a wound in the left hand. A bullet passed between the first and second finger, tearing both of them, and then passed through my top-coat sleeve without touching my arm. I'm in a rest hospital in Boulogne today, but expect to go to the base tomorrow, and then across to England within the next few days. I'm perfectly happy and being wonderfully well looked after, and it's quite possible that I might get a day or two's leave at home within the next week or so. As this letter may be*

A group of the 5th Battalion's NCOs and men in Hummersknott Camp, Darlington 1914.

opened I cannot say as much as I would like. I shall have lots of news to tell you when I get over, which I feel sure will be shortly.

Private Charles Linn was writing home from the British Soldiers' Buffet at Boulogne. He was shipped back from the front to the Auxiliary Military Hospital at Breeze Hill, Bootle, Liverpool. There he was put under the care of a Scarborough Matron, Miss McNaught, who had given up a career as a teacher to join the Red Cross. Before the war Charles was Secretary of the Scarborough Football Club. He is not listed as died.

From the base we went into the trenches for three days and had many casualties, including officers.

I was very lucky for I had a bullet go right through my pocket case, which was in my shirt pocket, and clean through my shirt and vest - and it never touched my skin! Also myself and three more chaps were absolutely buried in our trench when a shell hit the parapet. It did me no harm, but my rifle was badly smashed - which I found out afterwards. I am quite well, but, like many others I think England is the safest place!

At present we're at the rest camp and I don't know when we shall leave again.

Private Jack Drake was writing home to his parents in Roscoe Street. He is not listed as died.

Just a line to tell you I got wounded in the leg at 6.00am on Sunday morning. I am now in a hospital in Boulogne.

Don't worry about me I'm all right, though my leg is very painful.

I think I shall be in England by the time you get this. I've not heard of poor cousin Fred. I saw him on Saturday night. I will let you have a letter later.

Don't write back.

I have not received any parcel or letter.

A group of 5th Green Howards on garrison duty at West Hartlepool, the card is postmarked 31st August 1914.

Private J. Lambert was writing home to 60 Commercial Street, from a hospital in Boulogne. He is not listed as died.

His cousin, mentioned in the letter, Private Frederick Carter of 106 Prospect Road, was one of the Battalion's stretcher-bearers (these were generally Bandsmen in peacetime). He is not listed as died.

A LITTLE WET HOME IN THE TRENCH

I've a little wet home in the trench,
Where the rainstorms continually drench.
There's the sky overhead,
Clay or mud for a bed,
And a stone that we use for a bench.

~

Bully beef and biscuits we chew,
It seems years since we tasted a stew.
Shells crackle and scare,
Yet no place can compare,
With my little wet home in the trench.

~

Our friends in the trench o'er the way,
Seem to think that we've come out to stay.
They shoot and they shout,
But they can't get us out,
Though there's no dirty trick they won't play.

~

They rushed us a few nights ago,
But we don't like intruders and so,
Some departed quite sore,
Others left ever more,
Near my little wet home in the trench.

~

So, hurrah for the mud and the clay,
Which leads to Der Tag and the day,
When we enter Berlin,
That city of sin,
And make the fat Berliner pay.

~

Private
George Pearson.

Private
Ernest Baker.

Private
Robert T. Baker.

2023 Private
George Arthur Jude.

Yes we'd think of the cold slush and stench,
As we lay with the Belgian and French,
There'll be shed then I fear,
Redder stuff than a tear,
For my little wet home in the trench.

240314 Private Albert Megginson wrote this parody based on the popular 'Little Grey Home in the West'. He was born in Scarborough and enlisted there. He later went on to be promoted to Sergeant and earned the Military Medal. Albert survived until killed in action on the 28th October 1917, while in the front line area of Marsuin Farm in the Elverdinghe sector. He was 24. Albert is buried at the Tyne Cot Cemetery, Passchendaele, Belgium, and is commemorated on the Scarborough War Memorial.

Just a line to let you know that I'm safe and well. I had some narrow escapes of being killed with shells. Some of the lads of the 5th have, I think, gone under. I hope Will [brother] is going on all right. The countryside about here is greatly destroyed. We've been in the thick of it.

Private George Pearson was writing home to his mother at 1 Shield's Yard, Falsgrave. George joined the Regimental Band when he was only 9 years old. In 1915, at the age of 17, he was serving with the Battalion's stretcher-bearers. He is not listed as died.

His brother, Private William Pearson, also of the 5th Green Howards, was still at home in England very ill, hence George's enquiry about his wellbeing. Although he is not listed as died, the name W. H. Pearson does appear on the Scarborough War Memorial, and it is possible they are one and the same.

We've been up to the trenches for five days and we're in a resting place just now. We've been very lucky to get back without a scratch. The other night we had a bit of luck. A shell burst a few yards away from us and injured three or four more who were with us, and killed two horses. We've had a good many exciting moments in the last few days.

Men of the 5th Green Howards in camp 1915, before leaving for France.

Private Ernest Baker and Private Robert T. Baker (brothers) were writing home to their parents at 29 Tennyson Avenue. Neither of them is listed as died.

> *I'm in hospital wounded in the arms. They're taking me down to the base. Don't fret for I am feeling all right. Tell my mother about me. I will write a long letter as soon as I can and tell you where I am and how I'm getting along.*

Private Jude was writing to his wife at 3 Taylor's Yard, off Castle Road. The name Jude appears twice on the Scarborough War Memorial, though it is unclear if either of these is Private Jude. The only Jude listed as died with the 5th Green Howards was 2023 Private George Arthur Jude. He was born in Hull and enlisted at Beverley. He survived until dying of his wounds, at the age of twenty-two, on the 4th October 1915, while in the Armentières sector. George is buried at the Bailleul Communal Cemetery Extension, France.

NEVER MIND

If there's Germans over there, never mind.
If there's Prussians over there, never mind.
There's England, Belgium, France,
They'll lead them such a dance,
When they make a big advance, never mind.

~

If you think this song is rot, never mind.
It's all the sense I've got, never mind.
There's our other Allies yet,
They will do their share, you bet,
And they'll make old Billy sweat, never mind.

~

If this little song hurts you, never mind.
It's as good as I can do, never mind.
When the troops of ours you know,
With the bayonet start to go,
They will lay the Germans low, never mind.

~

RSM Radley and Major C. H. Pearce in dug-outs, April 1915.

I hope you won't take fright, never mind.
While this other bit I write, never mind.
When the Kaiser's men in mass,
Try to wipe us out with gas,
We'll drive them back with brass, never mind.

~

There's just a little bit more, never mind.
So if your heart is sore, never mind.
But I know it's a test,
For you to stick the rest,
So I hope you'll do your best, never mind.

~

I'm going to try again, never mind.
Some more to put to this, never mind.
I am sure you'll admit,
The 5th Green Howards have done their bit,
And are full of Britain's grit, never mind.

~

I've left a little out, never mind.
But I know you've no doubt, never mind.
Our officers when they lead,
Never shirk a daring deed,
They are full of English breed, never mind.

~

We've a Captain here you know, never mind.
Who's won the DSO, never mind.
He showed the greatest pluck,
To his duty always stuck,
So we wish him the best of luck, never mind.

~

To finish up this song, never mind.
It'll not take me long, never mind.
Take advice from a friend,
We'll smash them in the end,
And be happy once again, never mind.

1912 Private Harry Webster wrote this little ditty for his comrades in arms, Privates Blagg and Costello who called themselves ***'The Nightingales of the 5th Green Howards'*** and who described themselves as

Two unnamed Green Howards Privates, in camp 1914.

'performing somewhere in France'. Harry was born in Scarborough and enlisted there. He survived until killed in action on the 16th September 1916, while on the Somme. He was 21. Harry is buried at the Becourt Military Cemetery, Somme, France, and is commemorated on the Scarborough War Memorial.

1825 Private Albert Costello was born in Scarborough and enlisted there. He also survived until killed in action, the day after his friend Harry Webster, on the 17th September 1916, while on the Somme. Albert was just 18. He is buried at the Adanac Military Cemetery, Somme, France, and is commemorated on the Scarborough War Memorial.

The third man in the trio is likely to be 30008 Private John William Blagg who was born in Mansfield and enlisted there. He had earlier served with the Nottinghamshire and Derbyshire Regiment, when his service number was 34057. John survived until killed in action on the 27th May 1918, during the great German offensive. He is buried at the Sissonne British Cemetery, Aisne, France.

PRO ABSENTES

Our absent lads are fighting,
In many a gory field,
For their King and Country,
And the cleanness of our shield;
Drawing the sword of justice,
So that our escutcheon proud,
With blot or sullification,
May not be endowed.

~

For us at home in England,
They're laying down their lives,
Forsaking home and kindred,
Children and weeping wives.
Then honour now the absent,
The heroes of our land;
May the God Almighty,
Bless their glorious band.

Captain Crockatt, the Battalion's third Adjutant, pictured at Armentières, November 1915.

This poem was penned by Scarborough youngster, Richard Clough, of 19 Holbeck Hill. The name P. R. Clough appears on the Scarborough War Memorial and one cannot help but wonder if there is a family connection.

> *You would see that the last letter was not written by me, because I was too ill to do anything, but now I am sick of lying here. Do not ask me the whereabouts of any of my pals, as I was one of the first to be wounded. We were roughing it, I can tell you. All we got to eat was corned beef and biscuits, which were as hard as iron.*
>
> *It would not be wise to send anything as I think I shall shortly be sent to England. I have lost everything, including razors and it's a fortnight since I last shaved!*

Private James Agar was writing home from Overflow Ward 13, General Hospital at Boulogne, to his parents at 77 Longwestgate. He is not listed as died.

> *It is the opinion of everyone here that this is the biggest battle of the war.*

Quartermaster Sergeant P. Foord was writing home to his wife from a stores depot close to the line. He survived the war and became a stalwart member of the Scarborough Branch of the Old Comrade's Association.

> *Thank you for the [Scarborough] Pictorial. We've had a rough time of it this week. No doubt you'll know by now that we've been in action and a very hot time we've had of it. We came under fire last Saturday and were hard at it until late last night. No one who has not been in it can possibly imagine what it's like. Our Battalion has done very well, though we've suffered a few losses. By degrees we got right up to the firing line, and I think we accounted for a few Germans.*

A Green Howards Pioneer.

I thought of Scarborough and of home while I was there, and did my level best to pay back a few scores. When shrapnel and 'Jack Johnsons' [a type of shell] are flying round you, you don't half think things. You cannot say you are frightened because it does no good being so. You are there to do your duty and that makes all the difference. We know what the Huns did at home after their half hour's bombardment, but to see poor Belgium after over eight months makes our blood boil. To see the dead and dying men and horses is terrible, but it only makes one more eager to get at the enemy.

We've only had one wet night while we've been out, but we slept out in an open field without a bit of trouble. It's very peculiar, but when in the trenches, and the firing is going on, it does not matter how fierce it may be, you can get a real good sleep without a bit of trouble.

Private Harold Merryweather was writing home to his parents at the Chapman Hotel, Blenheim Street. The Merryweathers had a daughter-in-law killed during the bombardment of Scarborough on the 16th December 1914. Harold was an organist at St John's Road Primitive Methodist Church before the war. He survived and in 1923 played a major role in the unveiling ceremony of the Scarborough War Memorial.

THE 5TH GREEN HOWARDS PIONEERS

There's a section of lads with the 5th Green Howards in France,
Who are worth something more than a passing glance.
They're here for hard work, fighting Huns ain't their game,
But they get in some very hot spots just the same.

~

No.1's, Sergeant Marlow, their leader and friend,
A brave Yorkshire laddie, the very best blend.
You won't find one better, wherever you stay,
Than this fine dashing non-com from down Scarborough way.

~

Wounded and invalids of the 5th Battalion resting in Scarborough after the Battle of St Julien.

No.2's, our old veteran, Joe Carr to wit,
Who's seen lots of service and travelled a bit.
A heart full of pluck and a good hand at nap,
A regular old sweat, but a real decent chap.

~

Then there's Freddy Ward, a terror for fun,
Who'll fight anyone from two stone to a ton.
Jimmy Watson, the cure, full of practical jokes,
Jack Barnet, George Whitelaw, two long service blokes.

~

The last mentioned two, a real plucky pair,
Of good Yorkshire grit they have got a fair share.
At straight honest toil we all know their worth,
You couldn't find two better pals on God's earth.

~

Then comes Tommy Carter, a young 'un, but game,
Tending the stew he's got a good name.
Joe Bradley, a good 'un, whose nickname is Brad,
A good honest worker, a Beverley lad.

~

Then we have Charlie Porter, who's one of the best,
Always willing to do his full share along with the rest.
A lad full of fun and of this there's no doubt,
You cannot feel glum when old Charlie's about.

~

The next is eight-yard Shilbeck, who I'd like you to know,
Was wounded in France just a short time ago.
He's gone back to Blighty across the wide main,
But we hope that he'll soon be amongst us again.

~

There's Fawbart and Mac, the two lads full of grit,
Who've been invalided home after doing their bit.
Two bright Yorkshire lads of the very best strain,
And we all wish them luck till we see them again.

~

Now I've mentioned each one of this brave little band,
All are doing their bit for the dear old homeland.
So let's raise our hats and give three ringing cheers,
For those fine plucky lads of the 5th Pioneers.

5th Green Howards in camp 1914. Private Henry Richmond standing fourth from left, with a mallet.

Private E. Dawson was writing from 'somewhere in France' with ringing praises for his fellow pioneers, the 'diggers' of the Battalion. He is not listed as died. [On the 16th November 1915, with the forming of specific Pioneer battalions, the 7th Durham Light Infantry, from the 151st Brigade, became the 50th Division's Pioneer Battalion.]

3481 Private Frederick William Ward from Low Farndale, Kirkbymoorside, enlisted at Scarborough. He survived until killed in action, at the age of twenty-two, on the 2nd March 1916, while in the area of Sanctuary Wood. He is buried at Maple Copse Cemetery, Belgium.

Sergeant Marlow's home was given as 4 Niso Terrace (although this may be an error), but he, along with the other men mentioned above, is not listed among the Battalion's dead.

> *I'm living and all right, much to my surprise! We've been five days in the trenches and God only knows how I came out. I think I was born lucky - it was hell upon earth. Every eligible young man ought to come out and help squash the job. The Canadians are splendid fellows. They'll not be choked off once they're set going, and they say they're proud to have been with the 5th Green Howards. They don't half praise us up. They've christened us 'the Fighting Gurkhas'.*

Private A. E. Dove was writing home to his wife at number 2 Mile End Cottages. During the summer of 1915 he was wounded in the thigh and leg and was shipped home to the Royal Infirmary at Sunderland. He is not listed as died.

> *Had an awful time for five or six days and nights, as fighting seldom ceases, and one day got mixed up with another. We've had several casualties, but were wonderfully lucky, and I'd only about three hits of shrapnel myself, two small and one a bit strong, which struck a fleshy part and only cracked the skin. It's like a return from hell itself to be here at the rest camp, although we're under shellfire, wet and are even now having to dig*

Wounded and new recruits of the 5th Battalion in Bridlington after the battle of St Julien.

'funkholes'. We were at the front in the thick of the fighting before we had time to realise it about a week ago. Very sharp work from leaving England. Our Battalion behaved like veterans. And got a very good name, but we lost a fair number of poor chaps.

Last Sunday was a terrible day. How anyone was missed among tons and tons of shot and shell was marvellous. We took part in a great battle at a place already famous for hard fighting, but men who were at Neuve Chapelle and other places say this was the most terrific they'd endured. We were two days and nights in the open, and slept where we knocked off at dusk, though shellfire continued, but the next night we dug ourselves in and have been entrenched ever since.

The sights of this war must beat anything yet seen, and you have a faint idea of it in Scarborough, seeing the destruction there, but here you see not a single building left whole in town, village or countryside and added to that, other things, that must necessarily result from such destructive fire - the scene beats description. We've got relieved from the front trenches for a day or two. And that is how I'm able to write and get letters through, as it's almost impossible to get them to us. I saw one lot scattered about the road, where some poor fellow had come to grief in an endeavour to get his mates' letters through.

I call to mind that Mrs Crawford asked me to send names of Scarborough men so that she could send them parcels of clothing, but our kit is so heavy, as we carry blanket, top-coat, and everything we use, that heaps of good things are littering the road, and though one should not choose a gift, of course the most needed thing we've wanted is a good drink of tea, which we could not get for a few days as fires were shelled as soon as lit.

From left to right: Sergeant Bennison, Corporal Carr and Corporal J. W. Bielby.

Bandsman Fred Carter.

2277 Private A. George Harold Bradley.

How I blessed the Huns! But anything in the nature of chocolate would be most useful, as its weight would soon get less; but for my part I don't think it worthwhile sending much of anything as moving about so much one might not get them.

Corporal Thomas Little was writing home to his wife at 1 Palace Hill. Thomas, an experienced NCO, saw 30 years' service, first with the Green Howards Volunteers, with whom he served in South Africa, and then with the Green Howards Territorials. He is not listed as died.

I've been admitted into Boulogne hospital, having been struck on the side of my left eye, and also a shrapnel wound under my right ear. They succeeded in extracting the piece of shrapnel yesterday morning and I'm now feeling more comfortable. I hope to cross over to England tomorrow.

Private Frederick Horton, aged 21, was writing home from hospital in Boulogne to his parents at 10 Greenfield Road. Fred was the youngest of three brothers. Before the war he worked for Land & Co., on South Street, Scarborough - bombed during the 1914 bombardment and severely damaged. He is not listed as died.

His elder brother, 7097 Lance-Corporal Douglas Horton, served with the 18th (Queen Mary's Own) Hussars - part of the original British Expeditionary Force. He was born, and later enlisted, in Scarborough. Douglas was killed in action on 20th October 1914, and is commemorated on the Scarborough War Memorial.

At the time of Fred Horton writing to his parents they had still not heard anything from, or about Douglas.

Sorry to say I've had some bad luck. On the 25th I got wounded in my left leg with a shell. I'm now in hospital down at the base, but I'm progressing well. With a bit of luck I may get over to England. I think Harry [brother] is all right, although the 5th got it pretty hot.

Men of the 5th Green Howards signalling section at rest after the Battle of St Julien.
Left to right, front: C. Rudolph Duthoit, J. Knaggs and Lance-Corporal Ruston
Left to right, back: F. Lyons, F. Henham and W. Dawson.

Private George Newby was writing home to his parents at 66 St John's Road. He is not listed as died.

The brother whom he mentions in his letter is 2133 Private Henry Newby. He was born in Bridlington and enlisted there. He survived until dying of his wounds, aged twenty-three, on the 21st September 1916, while on the Somme. He is buried at the Etaples Military Cemetery, Pas de Calais, France, and is commemorated on the Scarborough War Memorial.

A third son of Mr and Mrs Newby, Ernest William Newby, served with a Bantam Battalion. He died during the war and is also commemorated on the Scarborough War Memorial.

> *We are returning to the rest camp after six very hot days in the first line. Sorry to say my pal Fred Horton has been wounded in the face; I don't know whether serious or not. I lost him in the general confusion. We had to take up the offensive. Everyone has described our work as immense. If we'd not stuck to the attack things in this, one of the fiercest parts of our line, would have been most serious for us. We are known here as the 'English Gurkhas'. Their German stink bombs made our eyes water terrific. Vasey is all right. I have not come across Harry Bradley though.*

Private C. Rudolph Duthoit, a Signaller with the Battalion, was writing home to number 2 The Esplanade. He is not listed as died.

2277 Private A. George Harold Bradley is mentioned at the end of the letter. He was born in Scarborough and enlisted there. His home was at 5 Royal Avenue. Harry was wounded and shipped back to England to a nursing home in Huddersfield. He later died of his wounds while at home (probably in hospital) on the 18th May 1915, not yet having reached twenty-one.

Harry was buried in the town with full military honours and hundreds of people attended the funeral. The coffin, draped in the Union Flag, and topped with wreaths, was drawn on a bier with an escort of bearers from the Battalion. Both the firing and the bugle party were drawn from the Northern Cavalry Depot on Scarborough's Burniston Road. [The Burniston Road barracks no longer exist -

Left to right:
Company Sergeant Major Jack Brammall,
Corporal Parker and Sergeant Bradley.
The three men are pictured outside Scarborough railway station about to return to the front after spending a weekend at home after the Battle of St Julien.

replaced in recent years by a vast modern housing estate.] In the wake of the cortège marched detachments from the 5th Battalion, the Royal Field Artillery and the North Riding Regiment of Volunteers. Harry is buried at the Manor Road Cemetery and is commemorated on the Scarborough War Memorial. However, his name and place of burial are not recorded in the *'Casualty Listing'* for the 5th Battalion.

2948 Private Frederick Vasey is also named in the letter. He enlisted at Scarborough, and survived until killed in action on the 11th April 1916, while in the Locre area. He was 20 years old. Fred is buried at the Lindenhoek Chalet Military Cemetery, Belgium, and is commemorated on the Scarborough War Memorial.

> *Just a line to let you know I'm all right, but my pal Ted [Hardcastle] has been shot through the elbow. We're just about getting used to shrapnel and shells now. I've been guarding the ammunition and ration transports and also escorting them up to the trenches.*

Private Ware was writing home to his mother at 11 Hanover Road. He is not listed among the dead of the 5th Green Howards. However, it may be, as he enquires about his friend Ted Hardcastle from Malton (who is not listed as died), that this is 204024 Private Frank Ware, of Malton, who died at home on the 30th November 1917, presumably of wounds sustained while serving with the 4th Green Howards in the Elverdinghe area. [Due to reorganisation many men from the 5th Battalion were moved to the 4th Battalion towards the end of the war.] He is commemorated on the Malton War Memorial. Frank is believed to be buried at Malton, however, his name and place of burial are not recorded in the *'Casualty Listing'* for the 5th Battalion.

NUMBER TEN PLATOON OF THE 5TH GREEN HOWARDS

Now, as I'm not busy and have some spare time,
I'll endeavour to compose a topical rhyme.
I will start with the Captain, who's one of the best,
And try to mention a few of the rest.

A group of 5th Green Howards hard at work at Hartlepool, following the German naval bombardment of the town on 16th December 1914.

Well, Captain Scott is a real good man,
And aims at helping us all he can.
The Scarborough lads all wish him much luck,
And one and all admire his pluck.

~

Next we come to Lieutenant Bagge,
He's a good sort you never hear brag,
While on patrol he's fearless and true,
And with good luck we hope he'll pull through.
Then comes Jack Brammall, our popular S.M.,
Whose name appeared in an 'Evening News' 'mem',
In civil life he is well known in sport,
And as a soldier is a very good sort.

~

Now, Brookie's a Sergeant, a nice little chap,
It's not the first time he has been in a scrap,
For he fought with the Howards on Africa's sand,
And is never found wanting, and is always at hand.
Now we come to Alex, a Beverley lad,
If he was made Sergeant all would be glad.
Next is old Bobs, a full Corporal too,
He's not a bad sort, to give him his due.

~

Of Lance-Corporals we have quite a lot,
And one in particular must not be forgot.
This comrade is Reg, one of five,
All with the colours and still alive.
Next we have Dunn, a big strapping chap,
Who'd never be missing if we had a scrap.
Then we have Pickup, from Houghton-Le-Springs,
When in the trenches many rumours he brings.

~

Now there is Jack, from Seamer town,
A real good soldier up and down.
Then we have Gibson, a moulder by trade,
For work in the trenches a name he has made.

Captain George Jefferson Scott, pictured before the war at one of the 5th Battalion's annual summer camps.

The last of our non-coms is Johnson by name,
Although only a youngster he is playing the game.
Now for the Privates from this good old town,
We have quite a lot very well known.

~

There's Mumford and Marshall and Megginson too,
All Scarborough lads, both steadfast and true.
Indeed, so many from each different part,
That I don't know exactly just where to start.
But there's Richie from butterscotch town,
Who'd give a smile rather than frown.
There's young Bill Brown from Loftus town,
And Tom the wild moor's own.

~

There's Casey and Harry, both well-worn vets,
Always ready with jokes and jests.
And there's Oliver too from Bridlington Prom,
Who laughs and still keeps plodding along.
Then comes John Watson from Norton, near York,
And Vasey, a tall lad from somewhere up north.
Next come Archer, Appleyard and Mick,
Three lads to whom luck seems to stick.

~

Jarvis and Senior are the very best of chums,
And would stand by each other right up to the guns.
Count Stevenson, Stead and your humble as well,
Then I think I have no more to tell.
I've mentioned the lot who are here with us now,
And perhaps after this I'll be in for a row.
But it's all done for fun, as all will agree,
And all such sport free from censure should be.

~

Now this is the lot in Platoon number ten,
And I close with good wishes from all of the men.
For your paper is good and your kindness great,
I hope you'll insert this if not too late.
So, here's to the 5th Green Howards and Platoon number ten,
Almost entirely composed of our Scarborough men.

2234 Private James Richard Stevenson, September 1914.

Private W. Stonehouse, with the help of other men of the Platoon, wrote and sent the preceding rhyme to the local [Scarborough] paper. He is not listed as died.

Captain George Jefferson Scott, from Market Weighton, near Driffield, had been with the Territorials for some time before the war. He was mentioned in despatches and survived until killed in action on the 25th December 1915, while in the trenches at Dickebusch. He was 41 years old. The loss of Scott was greatly felt by those who had served with him. He is buried at the Poperinghe New Military Cemetery, Belgium.

Lieutenant H. P. Bagge joined the Battalion in France shortly after the Battle of St Julien. He is not listed as died. Neither are any of the following men; Sergeant-Major Jack Brammall, Lance-Corporal Dunn, Lance-Corporal Pickup, Private Herbert Mumford of 11 Market Street, Private William Brown, Private Appleyard and Private Senior.

Private Rupert Stead was the son of the Seamer Stationmaster. He is not listed as died.

Private A. Marshall hailed from Tindall Street. Although he is not listed among the Battalion's dead, the name A. H. Marshall appears on the Scarborough War Memorial.

It is thought that the Gibson mentioned is 240265 Harold Gibson, who was born in Malton and lived, with his wife, in View Terrace, Middlecave Road. Harry enlisted at Malton. He was promoted to Sergeant and survived until killed in action on the 25th March 1918, while in the area of Licourt. He was 33 years old. He is commemorated on the Pozières Memorial, France, and on the Malton War Memorial.

1696 Lance-Corporal William Johnson was born in Scarborough and enlisted there. He survived until killed in action on the 10th January 1917, while in the Baizieux area. He is buried at the AIF Burial Ground, Flers, Somme, France, and is commemorated on the Scarborough War Memorial.

In the above verse NCO Johnson is referred to as a '*only a youngster*' and his age, at the time of his death, is given in the '*Casualty Listing*' for the 5th Battalion as 16. If this is correct then William was just 14, going on 15, at the time of the Battle of St Julien and must have been one of the youngest Green Howards to see active service during the war.

Private
R. Race.

240442 Lance-Corporal
Reginald Hollingsworth.

240481 Private
Charles E. Hebbron.

Private
Herbert Mumford.

2970 Private Thomas Harry enlisted at Scarborough and survived until killed in action on the 25th May 1918, during the great German offensive. He was 30. Tom is commemorated on the Menin Gate Memorial, Ypres, Belgium, and on the Scarborough War Memorial.

240541 Private John Reginald Oliver was born in Bridlington and enlisted there. He survived until killed in action, aged twenty, on the 15th September 1916, while on the Somme. He is buried at the Adanac Military Cemetery, Somme, France, and is commemorated on the Bridlington War Memorial.

240384 Private John Reginald Watson was born at Norton, near York, and enlisted at Malton. He was promoted to Lance-Corporal and survived until dying of his wounds on the 14th April 1918, while in the area of Chateau La Motte. He is buried at the St Sever Cemetery Extension, Rouen, France.

The Archer mentioned could have been either of the following men. 1709 Private George Archer was born in Scarborough and may have enlisted at Bradford. He survived until killed in action, aged thirty-three, on the 13th September 1916, while on the Somme. He is commemorated on the Thiepval Memorial, Somme, France. Private Herbert Archer was from Scarborough too. His home was at 91 North Street and in the summer of 1915 he was severely wounded in the head. He is not listed as died.

2001 Private William Earl Jarvis was born in Scarborough and enlisted there. He survived until killed in action on the 23rd June 1916, while in the Zouave Wood area. He was 21. William is buried at La Laiterie Military Cemetery, Belgium, and is commemorated on the Scarborough War Memorial

2234 Private James Richard Stevenson was born in Scarborough and enlisted there. He later earned the Military Medal, at Martinpuich on the Somme, in 1916. Jim was batman to both Major Brown (the Lieutenant H. Brown of the preceding narrative), and the infamous Colonel 'RED' Kent; an unusual character, apparently something of a dual personality, a cross between hero and villain. Jim was taken prisoner in May 1918, during the great German offensive and was finally repatriated at the end of December 1918. He died in May 1996, aged 101; his passing was marked by members of the Regiment, both past and present.

The only Casey listed among the Battalion's dead is 35665 Private Patrick Casey. He was born in Templemore, Londonderry and

Private Arthur Richmond, in 1914, one of three brothers to serve with the 5th Green Howards - all survived.

enlisted there. Patrick had earlier served with the Royal Inniskilling Fusiliers with the service number 27218. He survived until killed in action on the 27th September 1918, while in the Le Touquet area. He is buried at the Chauny Communal Cemetery British Extension, Aisne, France.

Private Megginson and Private Vasey are mentioned elsewhere in these pages.

> *I've had the misfortune to come up against a bit of 'Jack Johnson' [a type of shell] which caught me in the left arm. I am at present in hospital at Boulogne. Our Regiment has caught it very bad. We had five days in the trenches up to my being picked up, when the lads were just getting ready for a charge. On my way from the trenches I came through a town which was being shelled. It was a sight I shall never forget. There were buildings ablaze on all sides. Anyhow, now we are here we'll do our best.*

Private 'Ted' Edward Hardcastle was writing home to Malton. He is not listed as died.

> *We have had it very hot indeed. I'm still feeling very well, but a little shaken.*

240442 Lance-Corporal Reginald Hollingsworth was writing home to his parents at 41 Moorland Road. He was born in Flintham, near Bingham, Nottinghamshire, and enlisted at Scarborough. Reg survived until killed in action on the 12th April 1918, while serving with the 4th Green Howards in the Bethune area. [Due to reorganisation many men from the 5th Battalion were moved to the 4th Battalion towards the end of the war.] He is commemorated on the Scarborough War Memorial. Reg also had a brother, William, serving in the forces, though he is not listed as died.

> *I dare say you'll have heard by the time you receive this letter that we've been in the trenches for five days, and I can tell you, the first two days*

Private
John William Birley.

Private
Robert Edward Birley.

Private
Charles Linn.

Sergeant
Marlow.

we caught it hot. It was hotter than working in the retort houses at home.

We've come out of the trenches now for a few days, and we've earned it.

We are having warm weather here at present. It's far too hot for work of any kind.

We were with some French troops in the trenches the first day. They were dark skinned chaps. They gave us anything we wanted; chocolate, bread and hot tea, in fact they didn't know what to do to oblige us.

240481 Private Charles Edmund Hebbron was writing home to his father at 3 Mount Cottages, Seamer Road. Charles was born in Scarborough and enlisted there. He was promoted to Corporal, and survived until killed in action on the 15th December 1917. It is thought he was among those caught inside the 'C' Company HQ, in the Brandhoek area, when an enemy shell scored a direct hit. He was 23. He is buried at the Dochy Farm New British Cemetery, Belgium, and is commemorated on the Scarborough War Memorial.

You'll be glad to know I came through the action safe. We had five days without rest.

I had my knapsack off and lost all my things. I was struck in the back by shrapnel but it did not injure me. We were all the day under shellfire, and we held the first line of trenches for 24 hours. We were just about gasping for a drink of water at times. But we never lost heart and put a few bullets into the Germans whenever we could. They're cowards, they won't come out to fight.

Private R. Race was writing home to his parents at 34 Moorland Road. During the summer of 1915 he was wounded in the leg and was shipped home to a hospital at Chatham. He is not listed as died.

Within a week our Brigade [the 150th] has been into action in one of the fiercest battles, and I can say the lads have done splendidly. Of course, there

Major James Mortimer took over command of the 5th Battalion when Sir Mark Sykes was unable to travel through ill health. He was killed in action on the Somme in 1916, and his loss was greatly felt by all ranks.

have been a few casualties, but compared with the task undertaken they were small.

Sergeant E. Mason was writing home to his father in Norton, near Malton. He is not listed as died.

We've been in action for the last five days and have had a very hot time. We've been under fire the whole time and were not very well protected by the trenches. However you'll be pleased to hear we've made our name, for along with the Canadians we held a position after two other battalions had retired. Our Major [Mortimer] who was in command was splendid, and I for one would go anywhere with him. He has proved himself a man, and one of the best.

Of course we've had some losses and some of them you'll know. I'm sorry to say that both Captain Barber and Claude Dell were killed.

Captain Barber you will remember, was one of my favourites, and I feel it very much. Claude was only a foot off me and was shot through the head. I was awfully fortunate not to get hit, as about fifty of us got into a field and two Maxim guns opened fire on us.

I'm also sorry to say we've had other losses, but I'm not allowed to give a list. When the news came that the two battalions on our flanks were retiring Major Mortimer said very little, but it meant a lot: **'Yes, but the 5th Green Howards are not'.** *We held the position and were there for five days under a terrific artillery fire. Some of the regulars tell us it was worse than the retreat from Mons. We've been given the name of the 'Fighting Gurkhas' by the troops here. We were relieved last night and I can tell you we were about done in. We shall be well off for a day or two, as we're going to have a rest. The boys stuck it well and really deserve a rest.*

Private
Fred Horton.

1847 Private
Benjamin Watson.

Private
James Agar.

240314 Private
Albert Megginson.

[Later] Major Mortimer has just paraded us and given us a message from General Plumer. The General says he is very pleased with what we've done, and is sure that he can always rely on the Battalion to do its duty.

In case you don't hear from me for a day or two don't worry for we are not always able to write.

The Canadians are awfully nice chaps and will give us anything.

Corporal Stephen Davidson was writing to his best girl Miss N. Drake of Westborough. He is not listed as died.

Major James Mortimer, the Commanding Officer of the Battalion in the stead of Sir Mark Sykes, was born and lived in Driffield, East Yorkshire. He was promoted to Lieutenant-Colonel in 1915. Mortimer was greatly liked and respected by all those who served with him, and he was always keen with his praise of the men he commanded. Details about his earlier service appear in the preceding narrative. Mortimer survived until killed in action on the 15th September 1916, while moving up to lead an attack on the Somme. He was 45.

The *'History of the 50th Division'* states that he was killed in Pioneer Alley; however, this is incorrect. My Grandfather was close by when the officer was killed and records in his diary that ***'our Major Mortimer was killed by shellfire in Swansea Trench as we moved up'.***

Following Mortimer's death, command of the Battalion devolved on Major C. H. Pearce. Lieutenant-Colonel Mortimer is buried at the Flatiron Copse Cemetery, Somme, France.

We've been in the trenches for five days and had a pretty rough time of it, but I am still alive and kicking!

Private W. Daggett was writing to his relatives in Scarborough. He was born in America and is believed to be the only American to have served with the Battalion. He is not listed as died. It is believed that this is the same Daggett who, as a Sergeant, was the senior NCO with Captain Harold Brown's (a Lieutenant in the preceding narrative) party during the famous 1916 crater raid at Petit Bois.

Lieutenant Sleightholme, Captain F. W. Robson and Lieutenant F. Green (seated), Armentières, November 1915.

I'm sorry to tell you I've been wounded in the left shoulder bone by shrapnel. It about broke me in two. I was lying in the trenches together with a lot of our chaps. The German shells were absolutely whizzing round us and a lot of us were wounded. It rained heavily all our first day and we were simply wet through to the skin by night. We who were wounded were conveyed from the line by Red Cross ambulances and motor omnibuses. We've been out here a little over a week, but I feel like an old man of 60. I've not had a shave during that time so you can imagine the state of things.

Private John William Birley, aged 24, was writing home to his father at 83 William Street. John was one of three brothers serving with the forces. John was the eldest. He is not listed as died.

Private Robert Edward Birley also served with the 5th Green Howards. He is not listed as died. Nor is the third brother, Private Frederick James Birley of the 3rd East Yorkshires.

I'm writing to tell you I was wounded in the arm, above the wrist. The Germans were using poison shells against us. They nearly blinded us all, and then choked us. But we and the Canadians and the Scottish drove them back. Jim [brother] was all right when I left. They say it was the biggest fight there has been - those few days. We're looked after at the hospital like kings.

[Later letter.] Allow me to send a few words of sympathy to the wife of Private Smith, 5th Green Howards, of Cambridge Place, whose death I read of in the Mercury [the local paper]. He was a great comrade and I regret his death.

I am a lot better now myself.

1847 Private Benjamin Watson was writing home from the Red Cross Hospital in Beckingham, Kent, to his mother at 42 Hampton Road. He was wounded and shipped home to convalesce. Ben returned to Scarborough a few days after this letter arrived, about an hour earlier

632 Lance-Corporal
Claude Stanley Dell.

Second-Lieutenant
Charles H. Dell.

Private
A. E. Dove.

Private
Harold Merryweather.

than he was expected, thereby missing the welcome home that the town had planned for him at the railway station. The wound that Ben sustained at the Battle of St Julien, between the wrist and elbow, never properly healed and on 7th January 1916 he was honourably discharged from the Army after five years' service. After the war he married and continued to live in Scarborough, working on the railways. He died, aged 80, in February 1974.

81943 Private James Watson, Ben's elder brother, was born in 1870 and is believed to have lived for a time on the island of Guernsey. Later in the war he was taken prisoner and was finally discharged from the Army in January 1919. He spent the rest of his working life as a painter and decorator.

Another brother, William Watson, the middle one of the three, also survived the war.

724 Private James Smith, mentioned in Ben's later letter, was born in Scarborough and enlisted there. He was killed in action on the 21st May 1915, while in the Sanctuary Wood area. James is commemorated on the Menin Gate Memorial, Ypres, Belgium, and on the Scarborough War Memorial.

Please can you or your readers help me find and thank a young boy named Ben Watson of the 5th Green Howards, in action on 25th April at St Julien, for saving my life though severely wounded himself.

I was lying wounded in a farm used as a field hospital near Ypres when the Germans got the range and shelled the building so suddenly that within a quarter of an hour it was in ruins and on fire.

This boy, Ben Watson, seeing my danger came in and dragged me out under heavy fire. While he was so engaged about thirty others lost their lives. When I regained consciousness I was little the worse except for a piece of shrapnel through my chest.

He must have had a heart like iron. I hope he will soon be better, and once more I thank him from the bottom of my heart.

632 Lance-Corporal Claude Stanley Dell (right) and Sergeant-Instructor F. C. Sherwood.

Private S. Randell of the 2nd Battalion Montreal Canadian Division, was writing to the Daily Mail in an effort to find his brave rescuer, Private Benjamin Watson (he of the preceding letter). Subsequently the local paper printed his letter and Scarborough learned of Ben Watson's act of bravery - hence the reception which never was.

I understand from Ben's surviving relatives that a medal to honour his act of courage and bravery was to have been presented to him by the Canadians sometime after the war, but was never received, and nothing more was ever heard of it. After the war Ben attempted to contact Randell but his letter was never answered and one can only speculate as to the reason.

> *I'm writing to convey to you the sad news of poor Claude [brother] who met his end which was painless, and whilst doing his duty. Mr Brown, his Lieutenant, very kindly offered to recover his body and have it decently buried, and this I believe has been done. His wound was through the brain, and death was sudden.*
>
> *Guy and I are both scatheless, although I was hit in my pack by shrapnel, but the bullet did not go right through.*

Second-Lieutenant Charles H. Dell was writing home to his parents at 25 Londesborough Road [The *'Casualty Listing'* for the 5th Battalion gives his parents' address as 147 Falsgrave Road.] about the death of his brother, Lance-Corporal Claude Stanley Dell. He is not listed as died.

632 Lance-Corporal Claude Stanley Dell was born in 1889 in New Cross, Lewisham, Surrey, and enlisted at Scarborough. Before the war Claude had been a swimmer of note, having, along with his brothers, swum around the Castle Foot - no mean feat as Scarborians will know. He joined the Territorials in 1911. Twenty-six year old Claude was killed in action on the 25th April 1915, at the Battle of St Julien, Ypres, while with Captain Barber's party trying to take an enemy strongpoint. He is commemorated on the Menin Gate Memorial, Ypres, Belgium, and on the Scarborough War Memorial.

The third brother mentioned in the letter, Private Guy Dell also served with the 5th Battalion. He is not listed as died.

Wounded 5th Green Howards in Scarborough after the Battle of St Julien.

Two other brothers also served, one with the Royal Flying Corps in France, the other with the Yorkshire Hussars Yeomanry (Alexandra, Princess of Wales's Own). Neither of them is listed as died.

TO THE FIFTH GREEN HOWARDS

Ten short months ago, not more,
We watched them drill upon the shore;
Ah! Did we dream to see the day,
When they would enter in the fray.

~

They were so happy, young, and strong,
When on the march upon the 'Prom'.
That all the girls both sly and shy,
Were fain to turn and wink the eye.

~

They left us for a northern town,
Where they to work in trench got down.
But still they, with down-right good-will,
Said 'Come now, boys, let's show our skill'.

~

Some weary months they thus did spend,
But all for King and land defend;
With cheerful hearts they played the game,
Then at last 'the word' it came.

~

'Somewhere in France' the Fifth are going
The cry through street and foreshore blowing.
Ah, me! Our hearts were left an aching,
Mayhap, perchance, some fond one breaking.

~

They left us mourning on the shore,
Ah! We shall see some never more.
But we must needs endure our sorrow,
For 'duty first' has been their motto.

~

They faced the bayonet, shot and shell,
No flinching, though a comrade fell;

Second-Lieutenant Steuart Eberhardt George Corry was promoted from the ranks after the Battle of St Julien. As a Lieutenant he was killed in action on 26th June 1917, while leading an attack on an enemy position in Rotten Row trench in the Fontaine area.

For God, and Right, and Liberty,
They charged and won the victory.

~

How proud we feel for friends so brave!
How happy feels the wife that gave,
Her king to win such honour rare!
Let's hope he lives, with her to share.

~

Our daily, hourly, every prayer,
Is that each wife and sweetheart fair,
Shall in her arms her dear one hold,
Her darling, king, her hero bold.

This poem was signed simply 'Meg'; a regular contributor to the local paper.

> *The first night in France we spent in tents. It was awfully cold. We were up very early the next morning on that account. The day was spent in the camp until dark. When night came on we marched some miles and entrained for the front, close to the firing line. We did not go to the base at all. On arriving we marched several more miles to a farmhouse where we were billeted for two days. In the afternoon of the third day we were taken by omnibus to within a few miles of the firing line. After leaving the motors we marched to one of the many rest camps and expected to remain there for the night.*
>
> *We knew that we might be called on at any moment. This came sooner than we expected, and that same night we moved out behind the supporting trenches of the [French] Algerians, who were, owing to the asphyxiating gases, obliged to retire. That morning until daybreak we slept in the open, and on waking up found ourselves under heavy shellfire.*
>
> *It was there we suffered our first casualties, eight in number. The same evening we moved our*

Second-Lieutenant Leslie Hopper Rose was promoted from the ranks after the Battle of St Julien. During the war he was of able assistance to the Battalion's doctor, Dr Libbey, thanks to his pre-war chemist's background.

position, going towards Ypres, where the Canadians had taken their position. We advanced in the open without cover, under an absolute hurricane of shellfire. For so long that night we remained where we were until the order came to advance. We took up another position - also in the open - and I think most of the chaps were asleep when we were hurriedly roused up. We changed our frontage towards the position that was being held by an Irish Regiment. We remained the whole day under heavy fire. That was where the Adjutant and Captain Grant-Dalton was wounded.

Later when getting dusk we moved into the supporting trenches about 200 yards in the rear of the Canadians. That night we were fairly quiet. We remained there the next day and hoped to be relieved the same night, but this was not to be. We had to go on into the firing line and we stayed there until relieved, and jolly welcome we were to leave I can tell you.

On the Sunday previous to this was the day when Captain Barber, who distinguished himself by attacking a Maxim [machine] gun, met his death. Corporal Dell was also a victim. I do not want to give you any graphic description of the horrors of the fighting, because I might go on talking for a week, but as far as the first line of the 5th Green Howards is concerned I myself, and I think everyone who is with us, was proud to be in the battle.

The Commanding Officer, Major Mortimer, who acted with the greatest bravery and calm - as did all the officers - was obeyed absolutely and I think it was due to this and the discipline of everyone concerned that the Battalion came off as lightly as it did in the unprecedented circumstances.

On arriving back at the rest camp - where there is not much rest I can assure you - Major Mortimer addressed the officers, NCOs and men. He

*After being wounded at the Battle of St Julien,
Captain and Adjutant of the 5th Battalion, Stuart Grant-Dalton,
joined the Royal Flying Corps in January 1916
and, despite losing a foot after an aerial battle
with two enemy planes, he continued
flying throughout the rest of the war.*

explained to us that it was a forced necessity that called us into the trenches so early and he was greatly pleased in the manner in which every officer, non-commissioned officer, and man conducted himself, and he felt that after such a hard trial they were fit to take their part anywhere. Corporal Townsend, Corporal Rose and myself left the rest camp to cross over to England to make necessary arrangements to take up the positions of second-lieutenants and we were much envied by everyone.

There is no doubt that every officer, NCO and man is indeed a credit to the British Army and the town of his birth. I would particularly like to mention the name of Private Wright of the RAMC, who hails from Hull, who was shot through the head while attending to the wounds of a comrade. It was a most dastardly act on the part of a German sniper.

In conclusion I would like to say that our Battalion never faltered or failed in their attempts to hold our ground in the part of the line that was allotted to them.

Second-Lieutenant Steuart Eberhardt George Corry, newly promoted, was giving an interview to the local paper while at home; having attended an officer's training course prior to his promotion. The son of Dr Steuart Corry of Pavilion Square, Second-Lieutenant Corry was for some years a member of the Territorials before the war. He was described as an athletic young man who enjoyed football and boxing, as well as the less strenuous pastime of actor and vocalist with an amateur dramatic society. Corry, along with newly promoted Second-Lieutenant Rose, rejoined the Battalion in billets at Pont-de-Nieppe, near Armentières on 17th July 1915. Corry was further promoted to Lieutenant and survived until killed in action on the 26th June 1917, while leading an attack on an enemy position in Rotten Row trench in the Fontaine area. He is commemorated on both the Scarborough War Memorial, and the Arras Memorial in France. It should be noted that the official list of officers died lists him as

Captain Geoffrey Carew Barber was killed in action at the Battle of St Julien, 25th April 1915, while leading a party of men against an enemy strongpoint.
Twelve trees were later planted by local schoolchildren in his home village of West Ayton in his honour.

'Stewart-Corry' which is incorrect; Steuart was a Christian name and Corry his surname.

Second-Lieutenant Leslie Hopper Rose was the son of a local councillor. His home, above his parents' confectionery shop, was on South Street and he had a brother also serving with the Battalion. During the war he was of able assistance to the Battalion's Doctor Libbey, from Scarborough, thanks to his chemist's background before enlistment. He survived the war and eventually returned to his profession as a chemist. Rose died in 1939 just before the outbreak of the Second World War. By way of coincidence his son married the daughter of Captain E. Hilary Weighill, also of the 5th Battalion.

Captain E. Hilary Weighill, from Goathland, although with the 5th Battalion from the outset of the war, found himself, along with a handful of men, detached from the main force when they left for France in April 1915 due to being on garrison and guard duties at Scarborough and other north-east towns. These men then travelled to Newcastle where they joined the 2/5th Green Howards (the second line of the Battalion) until journeying to France after the Battle of St Julien as reinforcements. [It should be noted that the 2/5th never saw active service as a single entity, i.e. as a battalion in its own right, rather, drafts of men were transferred from it to the 1/5th as reinforcements and replacements as and when required.] Captain Weighill served until taken prisoner at Craonne Hill in 1918. Unable, because of his poor health, to return to his career as an engineer, he was for a time between the wars a Special Constable in the West Ayton district of Scarborough. He died on the 30th May 1979, aged 87, never havng regained his previous full strength or fitness.

Second-Lieutenant Guy Story Townsend was promoted to Lieutenant and survived until killed in action on the 23rd August 1918, whilst on attachment to the Machine Gun Corps. He is buried at the Bonnay Communal Cemetery Extension in France.

1532 Private Clarence Wright, of the Royal Army Medical Corps (Territorial Force), was born at Sculcoates, Yorkshire, and enlisted at Hull. He was killed in action, as described above, at the Battle of St Julien, 24th April 1915.

Captain and Adjutant Stuart Grant-Dalton was born in Bournemouth on the 5th April 1886. An experienced soldier, he was wounded on the 25th April 1915, at the Battle of St Julien, during the Second Battle of Ypres and took no further part in the fortunes of the

Captain E. Hilary Weighill - although with the 5th Battalion from the outset of the war - was one of the handful of officers chosen to form the cadre for the 2/5th Green Howards (second line of the Battalion from which replacements were sent). He joined the 5th Battalion on the Western Front shortly after the Battle of St Julien.

5th Battalion. After returning home to convalesce he joined the Royal Flying Corps in January 1916, and served as a 'flyer' for the rest of the war. In August 1916 he was wounded again during a mid-air fight with two enemy planes. The wound was so bad that he lost a foot. He rose eventually to the rank of Wing-Commander. Grant-Dalton earned the Distinguished Service Order (with clasp), the Air Force Cross, the Order of the Nile (4th Class) and was three times mentioned in despatches. Despite his many close encounters with death and injury he survived the war.

Captain Geoffrey Carew Barber was born in Scarborough in 1891. His father was the manager of the Nesfield Brewery and was on the town's Board of Guardians where he represented the village of West Ayton. Educated in the town, Barber left to attend Oakham College, and from there he returned to be articled to local solicitors, Watts, Kitching and Donner of Queen Street. He joined the Territorials in 1909 as a Second-Lieutenant. In 1913 he was *'gazetted'* Captain. In the summer of 1914 Barber passed his final solicitor's exams, and then went into summer camp with the 5th Battalion in Wales. Before the outbreak of war he had planned to undertake further study in London, but when the Battalion was embodied he remained with it. [Territorials were ***'embodied'*** for war, while the Regulars were ***'mobilised'***.]

Captain Barber, a well-liked and amiable man of 24, was killed in action on the 25th April 1915, at the Battle of St Julien, Ypres, while attempting to take an enemy strongpoint. He is commemorated on the Menin Gate Memorial, Ypres, Belgium, the Eleanor Cross, Sledmere, the Ayton Village War Memorial and on a brass plaque on the east wall of the south aisle of St Matthew's Church, Hutton Buscel - placed there by his family in 1919 in honour of him and his brother.

In 1915, on the 11th December, twelve trees were donated by Mr H. E. Donner and planted in the village in memory of Barber by local schoolchildren. Beneath the roots of each tree was placed a bottle containing a scroll with the name of the planters on it. The trees were dedicated by the Reverend F. G. Stapleton, Vicar of Seamer, who expressed the hope that the trees would become known as ***'Geoffrey's Avenue'***. Sadly however, thanks to road improvements and widening schemes, the original trees no longer stand, but instead were replaced with young trees along the central reservation of the road running westward out of West Ayton (the A170).

Private
George Newby.

Corporal
Thomas Little.

2034 Private
Frederick 'Leo' Hunter.

Private
J. Lambert.

As a mark of respect, and in an effort to keep faith with that original sentiment, I record below the names of those schoolchildren who planted the original twelve trees that their names may remain linked to Barber's memory.

1: *Mary Megson, Elsie Berryman and Ida Gibson.*
2: *Lilian Brown, Edith White and Alice Riley.*
3: *Agnes Raine, Irene Berryman and Edward Simpson.*
4: *Margaret Barraclough, Lilian Hebblethwaite and Kitty Rymer.*
5: *Elizabeth Fletcher, Kathleen Clark and Lawrence Rymer.*
6: *Marguerite Wilkinson, K. Raine, Alec Sawdon and G. Warcup.*
7: *Rhoda Berryman, Ina Stephenson and Edward Sawdon.*
8: *Freda Ward, Florence Wilkinson and Willoughby Raine.*
9: *Frances Warcup, Elsie Hill and Ada Prince.*
10: *Bertha Marshall, Mabel Cockerill and Arnold Berryman.*
11: *Hannah Theasby, Nellie Hebblethwaite, Hannah Marshall and Wilfred Cockerill.*
12: *Violet Gibson, Herbert Cockerill, Ada Fletcher and Vera Clark.*

Both of Barber's younger brothers also served during the war.

Lieutenant Frederick H. H. Barber served with the 5th Green Howards from the outset and survived the war.

Lieutenant John Byron Barber saw action in the Dardanelles with the Royal Navy aboard the destroyer HMS 'Bulldog'. He survived until killed by a mine explosion on the 16th April 1916 off Gallipoli and is commemorated on the Ayton Village War Memorial, the brass plaque in the church at Hutton Buscel, and on the Chatham Naval Memorial.

> *I suppose you'll have guessed we were at Ypres. We went straight into the firing line on Thursday. I can tell you we got it hot, as we were under shell-fire all the time. I'm sorry to say I got knocked out on Sunday morning with a shrapnel bullet. I've got the bullet with me, as it went through my left elbow and just grazed my ribs. A rifle bullet grazed my right elbow.*
>
> *Our Company was the first to advance and it was broad daylight and they just had the range of us with their 'Jack Johnsons' [a type of shell] and*

Major Cyril Harvey Pearce (right) with the Reverend Wolferstan (seated) and Dr Libbey (centre) pictured in their farmhouse billet on the Western Front, April 1915.

shrapnel. I'm pleased to say I got a few in at the Germans before I got knocked out. I'm sorry to say I lost everything. You see we had our full packs on. We were in the thick of it and when I got knocked out I had to leave my pack or get taken prisoner, as just at the time the Germans were advancing in mass. I'd to make my way back to get my wounds dressed, and of course I was under shell and rifle fire at the time. I fell dozens of times and at last came across some stretcher bearers, and they carried me into a blacksmith's shop in Ypres and the Germans were shelling it. It was just a bit rotten lying there waiting, expecting a shell to drop in at any moment. With a bit of luck I got safely away and I have not anything left.

Private Tate was writing home to his wife from a hospital in Lincoln. He is not listed as died.

April 17th: Left Newcastle 10.56am.
April 18th: Arrived at Boulogne 1.20am. Went into camp outside St Martin's Camp. One blanket each. Fifteen in a tent. Later left for Cassel in cattle trucks.
April 19th: Had a long march, about 12 miles. Arrived at billet. Could hear the guns. Wrote home. All well. Slept in a barn. On guard duty.
April 20th: On this day rested. Just mugged about all the time. The village is called Steenvoorde.
April 21st: Had a route-march round by water. Was again jiggered. Still here.
April 22nd:
April 23rd: Orders to shift in buses. Slept in rest camp.
April 24th: Left for trenches. Under fire all morning. Three chaps wounded.

2034 Private Frederick 'Leo' Hunter was writing in his diary. He was born in Hull and enlisted at Scarborough. His parents, of

The Signalling Company of the 5th Green Howards in camp, 1914.

49 Westborough [The *'Casualty Listing'* for the 5th Battalion gives their address as 109 Victoria Road.], were initially informed that he had been slightly wounded in the thigh. However, he died of those same wounds, sustained at the Battle of St Julien, on the 26th April 1915. He was 19. Leo is buried at the Poperinghe Old Cemetery, Poperinghe, Belgium, and is commemorated on the Scarborough War Memorial.

Four months later his belongings were returned; among them were his diary, cut short, and his camera with a partially exposed reel of film still inside. On developing and printing the film his parents discovered four, slightly clouded, photographs taken by their son which later appeared in the local paper. The first two pictures showed the tented camp at St Martin, the third the barn where Private Hunter was later billeted, and the fourth showed a group of 5th Green Howards with the Algerians in the trenches. [It should be noted that it was a serious military offence to possess a camera at the front.]

> *There appears to be some little misunderstanding with respect to the parcels of gifts which come out from Beverley for the men of the town.*
>
> *As your readers will remember, on Mobilisation the old 'C' Company of the 5th Battalion consisted almost entirely of Beverley men, and the Battalion was then of an eight company strength.*
>
> *However, some time before we went abroad the Battalion's formation was changed, in keeping with units of the Regular Army, into the present four company strength, and the old 'C' Company and 'D' Company (from Driffield) merged to form a single company, the present 'B' Company - which was under my command until I was appointed to my present position, when Captain Thomson took over from me. Owing to this change of formation and with men being transferred to other companies, and to various detachments, it is very difficult, and I might say almost impossible, to distribute gifts amongst men from any one place, as it takes considerable time to distribute when the men are together. We therefore try to divide*

A group of 5th Green Howards junior NCOs and men in camp, 1914.

everything as fairly as possible, and the last lot of parcels from Mr and Mrs Young I handed to the officer commanding 'B' Company, which contains most of the Beverley men.

Possibly some of the men may think this hard on them, but it is the best we can do, and these men perhaps benefit by sharing in gifts which have to be distributed under similar circumstances. I shall be very much obliged if you will kindly make this situation known through your valuable paper to our many kind friends in Beverley, and assure them that we do the best we can, and if every single Beverley man does not benefit, yet his comrades in his own Regiment do.

Major Cyril Harvey Pearce was writing to the local paper after grumbling at home about parcels not reaching the men they were intended for. Pearce had been with both the Volunteers and the Territorials for many years and was promoted Major shortly before leaving for France in 1915. An able officer, he went on to the rank of Lieutenant-Colonel when he took command of the Battalion following the death of Major Mortimer in 1916. On the 10th July 1917, while at the Quarry west of Cherisy, Pearce was wounded and Major J. A. R. Thomson assumed command of the Battalion (being promoted to the rank of Lieutenant-Colonel).

Colonel Pearce survived the war, serving for a time in Ireland in command of a battalion of the East Yorkshire Regiment. He later became Honorary Colonel of the 5th Green Howards, was awarded the CBE for his services to the Territorial Army, and was Deputy-Lieutenant of the East Riding. Pearce died in Bridlington on the 13th February 1943, aged 64.

WOUNDED 5TH GREEN HOWARDS AT SCARBOROUGH

Recovering here are the Yorkshire Gurkhas,
Who helped in the great advance,
To check the Germans at St Julien,
And the Huns, they hadn't a chance.

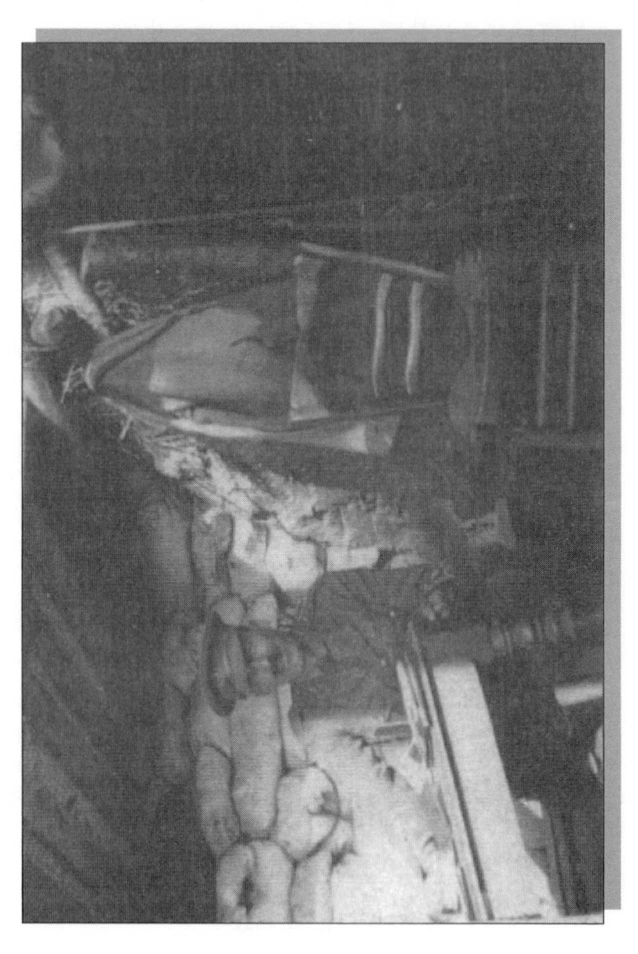

Lieutenant-Colonel James Mortimer, Commanding Officer, 5th Battalion Green Howards, in his Headquarters dug-out, April 1915.

~

One of the best lads on police was Bill Gray,
Another, a pal of his, Bill Brown,
And Jack Dunning and Teddie Green,
Four of the best lads in the town.

~

Now they're no longer policemen,
They're getting ready for France again,
Soon they'll be with the old Battalion,
Fighting with might and main.

~

We shall be sorry to part with the Gurkhas,
For some of them we hold dear,
But they want to be where the work's to be done,
Amidst the fighting . . . not here!

~

And when the old lads go back again,
Send them off with a right good will,
Proud to know they've done their duty,
And proud to do it still.

~

And when the new recruits go out,
May they strive with all their might,
To keep the grand name and example,
The old lads have won in the fight.

~

One thing I'm sure would look better,
For those who've had much to say,
If they'd had on their packs and their khaki,
And been with them to help in the fray.

~

Then give three cheers for the Gurkhas,
And let your voices ring,
For they all have left homes and happiness,
To fight for their country and King.

~

And when this war is over,
And the 5th Green Howards are home once more,

The 2nd Green Howards (Regulars) on parade prior to leaving for France in 1914 to join the BEF. By the end of October 1914 the Battalion, the first Green Howards to see active service, had been decimated during the First Battle of Ypres, its strength cut from over 1,000 to just 300.

They'll be proud to think they helped to keep,
The Huns from old England's shores.

~

Then here's to the Yorkshire Gurkhas,
You're a right good set and true,
Good luck we all must wish you,
Good health and troubles few.

~

And if ever you come back amongst us,
We'll do the best we can,
To play our part with a woman's heart,
For you have played the man.

Nora E. Cuthbertson of Esplanade Road, Scarborough, gave vent to her feelings about the brave lads she knew, and the shirkers she wished she hadn't. Of the men she names it is likely that they are the following members of the 5th Green Howards.

240165 Private William Henry Gray was born in Bridlington and enlisted at the 5th Battalion's drill hall there. He survived until dying of his wounds on the 11th March 1917, probably sustained several days earlier at the Second Battle of the Scarpe. He was 21. William is buried at the Etaples Military Cemetery, Pas de Calais, France, and is commemorated on the Bridlington War Memorial.

Of William Brown, Jack Dunning and Edward Green, none of them appear among the Battalion's dead.

We entered the trenches about midnight. We found them very uncomfortable, as there was only one single dug-out for our whole Company, and the officers were worse off than the men, for while they have a fire trench of their own we have nothing. We spent Friday trying to settle in.

The Germans were quiet, and Lieutenant Gorst tried to be polite by sticking up a sheet with 'Wellington-Blucher, 1815' on it, but all he got for his trouble was a dozen rifle shots through his sheet.

I spent about six hours making myself a shelter in a communication trench, a sort of sofa with a

240417 Corporal
John Henry Devlin.

Private
Herbert Archer.

240268 Private
Isaac Yaxley.

Private
Rupert Stead.

waterproof sheet above it, cut out of one side of a five foot trench.

It was icy cold last week, and I worked most of the night throwing earth up to shield my bed, as the Germans were sniping all our parapets all day long. Meals were wretched as we had nowhere decent to eat them, and we also lost our principal ration bag containing your tinned fruits and other joys. The place we did fix in got shelled the first meal, so we had to change.

On Saturday morning, coming off, standing to arms at 3.00am, the other officers turned in to sleep, and I stayed on duty until breakfast, reading the papers and letters. After breakfast I turned in for what I thought was to be an eight-hour sleep, but I was just in when a German shell burst about forty yards off, and whilst I was wondering whether I was safest where I was, or whether I should move into the fire trench, shell number two came straight at me. It was a high explosive shell for weakening trenches, and I think its nose went into the bank of soil I had dug overnight, for it pretty well buried me in light sandy soil and I got peppered on the left of the back and over the scalp. I fancy I was safer nearer the explosion than further off. I very soon found out I was not seriously hurt, and managed to get into the fire trench, where there were several men wounded out of my platoon. The Germans did not send more than about half a dozen shells, and then stopped and I was soon attended to. Private Yaxley, one of our own Scouts, put two field dressings on and helped to get me to the dressing station, and when there was no more room for the stretcher Majolier, another officer, and Corporal Milner, a Scarborough lad, carried me along finely. Doctor Libbey has just arrived out here, and he dressed me more thoroughly, and I lay on the stretcher in the dressing station till about 8.30pm, when

Lieutenants F. Green and Sleightholme and Captain F. W. Robson, Armentières, November 1915.

Privtes Yaxley and Dill (another of the Scouts) carried me down to meet the men from the motor ambulance.

It was the beginning of a rather weird journey. Every now and then a wagon with mules would be silhouetted against the sky, and lines of ration parties would file by. I was handed over to the first lot of stretcher men, who adjusted their respirators and mine, as they said the Germans were using gas shells. However, my respirator blew off, and at last we reached the road and the motor cars. Then a long journey began, broken up by two stages, one of about four hours and another of about six hours, at two receiving hospitals, at each of which I was dressed and my wounds cleansed a bit. The last section was taken by train, and then by stretcher and motor car to this hospital at Boulogne. It was all very tiring, with innumerable moves, and questions about my lost kit.

I started with the clothes I had on and ended in some flannel pyjamas, losing a suit and two waistcoats and pants along the way. I hung on desperately to my watch, even when I wanted my hand to get my weight off the stretcher.

The cobbled roads here are horrible, and what men suffer who have fractures I cannot conceive - a bad back is bad enough. At every shift, everything you have, boots, bundle, overcoat, are put on the top of you, and you are glad when the journey is in the open of the cool night air.

Well, I landed here about midnight on Sunday after 28 hours, the best part of which was in the train, where we had beds and two nurses, lemonade and tea. Only five cases were taken in here, and I was relieved to find I was to get off. I think because I was feverish.

The doctor here did not do anything till after his breakfast, and I had a sleep and some porridge for breakfast, and then the fun began again. I was

It was due to Sir Mark Sykes' belief in the Territorial Force that his troops were so well trained and disciplined. These men are pictured during exercises on the 'racecourse' at the 1912 Summer Camp at Scarborough.

whisked up to the x-ray rooms, and then straight into the operating room, and before you could say Jack Robinson I was under ether. Coming to in about half an hour, I found they had taken out a bit of shell, the size of a small bread bun from about an inch from my spine, so I had been providentially spared a bad wound. Another piece the size of a pea came out of my head. The rest of my wounds are just dirt and minute particles blown into me, and bruises.

We have every comfort here and nine nurses. All the ambulance arrangements seem very good.

Second-Lieutenant William Andrew Turnbull was writing home to his wife from hospital in Boulogne. The letter formed an account of his experiences for the avid readers of the local paper. Turnbull enlisted with the 5th Green Howards shortly after the outbreak of war as a Private and earned rapid promotion, reaching Second-Lieutenant only two months before leaving for France.

After being wounded he rejoined the Battalion at Sanctuary Wood in May 1915. In this area of the line he was to be wounded again, in early July, along with Lieutenant Gorst (mentioned in the above letter). He survived until killed in action on the 17th July 1916, while in the Locre area, where he was among a number of the Battalion's officers killed by enemy artillery fire. He was 37. Turnbull is buried at La Laiterie Military Cemetery, Kemmel, Belgium, and is commemorated on the Scarborough War Memorial.

Lieutenant Gorst, as previously stated, was wounded in early July while in the Hooge area of the line. He is not listed as died.

240268 Private Isaac Yaxley was born in Scarborough and enlisted there. He was wounded in the leg during the summer of 1915. Later he was promoted to Lance-Corporal and earned the Military Medal. He survived until killed in action on the 19th July 1917, while in the area of Dead Bosche Sap at Cherisy.

Isaac Yaxley was a close friend of my Grandfather, and they were together when Isaac met his death. On that day, after heavy action and having just repulsed a ferocious enemy raid, Jim records at the end of the day's account, quite simply, ***'My pal Isaac Yaxley was killed in Mallard Trench along with Corporal Devlin'.***

Machine-gunners, 5th Battalion. All are Privates, except where stated otherwise. Back, left to right: J. E. Cromack, W. E. Moore, G. A. Laybourne, W. J. Barrett and E. W. Putman. Sitting, left to right: J. R. Williamson, Corporal F. Dove, Sergeant T. Frankish and L. J. Moore. Floor, left to right: W. Swalwell, H. Wharton and F. Watson.

The following day Jim noted the burial of both men. Isaac is buried at the Heninel Communal Cemetery Extension, Pas de Calais, France, and is commemorated on the Scarborough War Memorial.

240417 Corporal John Henry Devlin was born in Scarborough and enlisted there. His home was at 76 North Street [The *'Casualty Listing'* for the 5th Battalion gives his parents' address as 13 Bedford Street.], and he began the war as a Private. As stated above he was killed in action on the 19th July 1917. He was 20. John is buried at the Heninel Communal Cemetery Extension, Pas de Calais, France, and is commemorated on the Scarborough War Memorial.

Second-Lieutenant E. Majolier temporarily took over as Battalion Adjutant following the wounding of Captain Grant-Dalton. He is not listed as died.

I have been unable to find any information on the other two men mentioned in Second-Lieutenant Turnbull's account; Private Dill and Corporal Milner.

There are three Milners recorded on the Scarborough War Memorial, but no Corporal Milner is listed among the Battalion's dead. Corporal H. Milner is recorded on the Bridlington War Memorial, but does not appear among the Battalion's dead. It is believed that this latter man, from Bridlington, is the one mentioned in the above letter.

> *It was whilst holding a reserve trench that what I consider a very brave deed occurred. On April 26th we were under the fiercest shellfire we have been under, when Private Johnson was struck in the leg by a piece of shrapnel, causing him a very dangerous wound. There were no stretcher bearers, and some of the men tried their best to stop the flow of blood, but couldn't manage it very well, as they had only very primitive material.*
>
> *We waited for about half-an-hour for stretcher bearers, or a stretcher, but neither turned up, so Private Chapman and Private Williamson, seeing Johnson in great agony, and losing a large amount of blood, volunteered to go and find a stretcher. They knew how awful the shellfire was, but still they went, and wandered about in search*

Left to right, back: Major C. H. Pearce, Captain G. J. Scott, Lieutenant F. Green and Second-Lieutenant E. M. Thompson, April 1915.

of a dressing station. After looking round for about an hour they found one three-quarters of a mile away. They got back safely and reported that they had been under fire from about half-a-dozen snipers (dressed in khaki), who were in a dug-out on the roadside. They were lucky to escape and thank God for their safety.

Now I come to the bravest part of the deed. The stretcher was brought, and four bearers were wanted. We were all very backward in volunteering, as their experience had impressed itself upon us so. However, Private Chapman, though dog-tired, said that he would go again if three more would go with him. Of course there were plenty of volunteers then, and three of the biggest chaps were picked.

When the four of them returned safely they all bore out Private Chapman's and Private Williamson's statement, and said they wouldn't go through it again for anything. What I consider made Chapman's deed so brave, was that he knew what he had to go through a second time. I am proud of him, and admit that if I had been in his place I don't think I should have gone through it twice.

This letter home, published in the local paper, was from an unnamed NCO.

240402 Private John Chapman was born in Hull. He lived at 34 Walkergate, Beverley and enlisted at the 5th Battalion's drill hall there. He survived until dying of his wounds on the 28th October 1917, while in the Marsuin Farm area. John was 22. He is buried at the Dozinghem Military Cemetery, Belgium. Despite John having been recommended for the Distinguished Conduct Medal by Major Pearce, following the above incident, there is no mention of the award having been made.

Neither Private A. Williamson, or Private J. D. Johnson is listed as died.

The wedding of Private F. Mason and Miss Ena Crawford in Scarborough.

WHEN THE BOYS COME MARCHING HOME

Far across the sea in Belgium,
Where the deadly cannon roar,
There's a band of laddies fighting,
For the land that they adore.
But they know they're not forgotten,
And no matter where they roam,
There will be a welcome waiting,
When the boys come marching home.

~

When the boys come marching home,
T'will mean goodbye to sadness.
When the boys come marching home,
Aching hearts will turn to gladness.
Back to the dear ones waiting,
Never again to roam.
Oh, won't there be a jubilee,
When the boys come marching home.

~

When the war clouds gathered o'er us,
In the ranks they took their stand,
And they mean to do their duty,
For the King and Motherland.
By the side of brave Canadians,
They fought and won the day,
And their names will live in history,
When the clouds have passed away.

~

When the boys come marching home,
T'will mean goodbye to sadness.
When the boys come marching home,
Aching hearts will turn to gladness.
Back to the dear ones waiting,
Never again to roam.
Oh, won't there be a jubilee,
When the boys come marching home.

~

Left to right,
back:
Sergeant Sugden,
Private Stockdale,
Private Frankish
and
Corporal Preston.
Front:
Private Redhead
and
Private Lee.

From blue eyes tears were falling,
On the day they said goodbye,
Leaving Motherland and dear ones,
Out in France their luck to try.
But those eyes will shine with gladness,
There'll be joy across the foam,
When those gallant Yorkshire laddies,
Once again come marching home.

~

When the boys come marching home,
T'will mean goodbye to sadness.
When the boys come marching home,
Aching hearts will turn to gladness.
Back to the dear ones waiting,
Never again to roam.
Oh, won't there be a jubilee,
When the boys come marching home.

Private Ernest Dawson dedicated these verses to his pals in the Battalion. His friend, Bandsman J. Wheeler, sent them to the local paper with the following letter. Neither man is listed as died.

> *I have forwarded the verses and chorus of a little song, thinking it would prove interesting to the people of Scarborough to know that one of their own has found time to write and compose it while facing the Germans in the trenches in Flanders.*
>
> *The Scarborough men of the Battalion think a great deal of it, and having got the melody and the chorus off, it is nothing strange to hear them humming it while exposed to murderous fire from the enemy artillery.*

Lieutenant Harold Brown (seated) in 1914 with the men from Filey who went to war with him.

Of Those Mentioned in the Narrative, or Pictured in Photographs

Lieutenant Harold Brown, originally from Bristol, lived at Filey, on the Yorkshire coast, and had been with the Territorials some time. At the Battle of St Julien, he was second-in-command to Captain Barber on the raid against the farmhouse strongpoint. As a Captain he later led the 5th Battalion's famous crater raid at Petit Bois in May of 1916. Promoted to Major he earned the Distinguished Service Order, Military Cross and Croix de Guerre with Palm (from the French). Brown was killed in action, while attached to the 4th Battalion, on 23rd March 1918, in the region of Brie on the Somme. He was 39.

My Grandfather, Brown's batman for a time, remembered him as a very brave man who commanded great respect from those with whom he served. He is commemorated on the Pozières Memorial, Somme, France.

Major Arthur Euston served with the 4th East Yorkshires. He is not listed as died.

591 Sergeant David Graham Joy was born at High Hoyland, near Barnsley. He enlisted at Sand Hutton, near York, and was killed in action on the 25th April 1915, at the Battle of St Julien, Ypres. David is commemorated on the Menin Gate Memorial, Ypres, Belgium.

Captain B. M. R. Sharp served with the 4th East Yorkshires. He is not listed as died.

Lieutenant-Colonel Sir Mark Sykes was born in 1879 at Sledmere Hall, Sledmere, near Driffield. He was the eldest son of Sir Tatton Sykes. At the age of 18 he served in the South African/Boer War with the Volunteer Company of the Green Howards. In 1911 he rose to become Commanding Officer of the 5th Battalion. In 1913 he was elected as an MP. He served on 'the Staff' during the war, 1914-19.

Sir Mark was responsible for raising the 1,000 strong 'Waggoners Special Reserve'; volunteer drivers attached to the Army Service Corps.

Although Sir Mark did not go to France with the 5th Battalion, he had been on the Western Front in September 1914 on a fact-finding tour primarily aimed at seeing how his Waggoners were faring. On his return to England he and Lady Sykes (his wife), having already paid

Lieutenant-Colonel Sir Mark Sykes,
Commanding Officer of the 5th Battalion,
was unable to travel to France because of ill health.
By the time he had recovered he was prevented
from joining the Battalion by the War Office
who required his expert knowledge on the Middle and Far East.

for the Metropole Hotel in Hull to be converted into a military hospital, endeavoured to improve the medical arrangements at the battle-front. In October 1914 Lady Sykes, accompanied by several nuns, took charge of a 150 bed hospital in a château just 25 miles from the front. A month later she set up a 35 bed hospital in a villa in Dunkirk, and in a joint effort with the French Red Cross she brought over 5 doctors, 25 nurses, and scores of orderlies and drivers from the East Riding to her hospital at Villa Belle Plage. Lady Sykes continued her work in France until the summer of 1915 when army medical arrangements began absorbing such private ventures.

Meanwhile Sir Mark Sykes took personal charge of training his 5th Battalion in and around Newcastle, and remained with them until they left for France. After the war he erected Memorials to both the Battalion and the Waggoners at the village of Sledmere on the Yorkshire Wolds near Driffield.

He died from pneumonia on the 16th February 1919, while in Paris attending the Peace Conference. He was 39 years old. Sir Mark, 6th Baronet, Commander of the Order of St Stanislas (Russia), Order of the Star of Romania, is buried at St Mary's Church, Sledmere, and is commemorated on the Eleanor Cross, Sledmere.

Captain James Albert Raymond Thomson, born at Huddersfield, had the distinction of taking the Battalion's first prisoners at Hull in 1914, when he was placed in charge of interned German ships and their crews. He was later promoted to Lieutenant-Colonel and earned the Distinguished Service Order and Croix de Guerre (from the French). He survived until killed in action on the 27th May 1918, during the great German offensive. He was 42. Thomson is buried at the Vendresse British Cemetery, Aisne, France, and is commemorated on the Malton War Memorial.

The following men are not listed as died: Sergeant-Instructor F. C. Sherwood, Sergeant J. Moorhouse, Colour-Sergeant J. Hill, Sergeant-Major W. H. Wilson, Sergeant D. P. Tonks, Sergeant H. Brooksbank, Sergeant H. Hugill, Lance-Sergeant P. O. W. Edeson, Lance-Sergeant H. Bradley and Private F. Mason.

Second-Lieutenant Henry Stewart Lambert, from Bridlington, commanding 'A' Company of the Battalion, survived until killed in action on the 11th January 1916, while in the Sanctuary Wood area. He was 19. Lambert is buried at the Poperinghe New Military Cemetery, Belgium.

Lieutenant Stewart Lambert (seated fourth from right) in 1914, with the men from Bridlington who went to war with him.

2035 Lance-Corporal Ernest Jackson enlisted at Scarborough and survived until killed in action on the 25th May 1915, while in the Zouave Wood area. He is commemorated on the Menin Gate Memorial, Ypres, Belgium, and on the Scarborough War Memorial.

Of the machine-gunners the following men are not listed as died: Private J. E. Cromack, Private W. J. Barrett, Private E. W. Putman, Corporal F. Dove, Private G. Clarke and Private W. Swalwell (though this name does appear on the Scarborough War Memorial).

240174 Private Frederick Watson was born in Seamer and enlisted at Scarborough. He was promoted to Corporal and earned the Military Medal. Fred survived until killed in action on the 28th October 1917, while in the Marsuin Farm area of the Elverdinghe sector. He is commemorated on the Tyne Cot Memorial, Belgium, and on the Scarborough War Memorial.

1454 Private Harold Wharton was born in Scarborough and enlisted there. Harry survived until killed in action on the 27th September 1915, while in the Armentières area. He is buried at the Chapelle d'Armentières Old Military Cemetery, Armentières, France, and is commemorated on the Scarborough War Memorial.

550 Sergeant Thomas Lumley Frankish was born in Rillington and enlisted at West Sutton. He survived until dying of his wounds on the 24th June 1915, while in the Zouave Wood area. He was 22. Thomas is buried at the Bailleul Communal Cemetery Extension, France.

240334 Sergeant Robert Williamson, of 'C' Company, was born in Beverley and enlisted at Scarborough. He survived until killed in action on the 28th March 1918, while in the Vrely area. He was 26. Robert is commemorated on the Pozières Memorial, Somme, France.

1943 Private George A. Laybourne enlisted at Scarborough. He survived until his death on the 28th May 1915, while in the Zouave Wood area. He was 20. George is commemorated on the Menin Gate Memorial, Ypres, Belgium, and on the Scarborough War Memorial.

1995 Lance-Corporal Henry Richmond was born in Scarborough in May 1892. He lived on Albion Street and enlisted in the town. Although with the 5th Battalion from the outset of the war, he found himself, along with a handful of men, detached from the main force when they left for France in April 1915 due to being on garrison and guard duties at Scarborough. These men then travelled to Newcastle where they joined the second line of the Battalion, the 2/5th, until journeying to France after the Battle of St Julien as reinforcements.

From left to right: Private A. Marshall,
Private Arthur Richmond and Private G. A. Hill.

Henry rose to Sergeant and survived the war to set up his own painting and decorating business. He died in Scarborough on the 14th September 1970.

Of Henry's two brothers, also with the 5th Battalion, Private Arthur Richmond, born in 1894 as twin to sister Emily, went out to France with a reinforcement draft from the 2/5th Battalion shortly after the Battle of St Julien. He survived the war, but suffered severely with shell-shock for the rest of his life. The third and eldest brother, Private John Thomas Richmond, born in 1889, was wounded on the Somme in 1916, though he too survived the war. He died in Scarborough on the 8th November 1961, aged 72.

36379 Private William Moore was born in Scarborough and enlisted there. He survived until killed in action on the 26th March 1918, while in the Craonne Hill area during the great German offensive. William is buried at the Pargny British Cemetery, Somme, France. The name C.W. Moore appears on the Scarborough War Memorial and it is believed they are one and the same.

3965 Thomas J. Mainprize enlisted in Scarborough. He survived until killed in action on the 13th September 1916, while on the Somme. Thomas is buried at the Flatiron Copse Cemetery, Somme, France, and is commemorated on the Scarborough War Memorial.

Captain Edward George Clarkson Bagshawe survived until killed in action on the 20th July 1916, while serving in the Locre sector. He was 36. Bagshawe is buried at La Laiterie Military Cemetery, Kemmel, Belgium.

Captain A. Perl, attached to the 5th Battalion from the Royal Army Medical Corps, is not listed as died.

Captain J. B. Purvis was the father of G. B. and J. S. Purvis. Before the war he was a chemist in Bridlington and this stood him and his men in good stead when the 5th Battalion first encountered the enemy's gas, for Captain Purvis recognised it for what it was and advised the men accordingly, no doubt saving many of them from serious injury, or worse. He survived the war.

Second-Lieutenant George Bell Purvis, from Bridlington, was promoted to Captain and survived until killed in action on the 8th June 1917, while on attachment to the 56th Machine-Gun Company. He is buried at the Klien-Vierstraat British Military Cemetery, Kemmel, Belgium, and is also commemorated on the Bridlington War Memorial.

Left to right, back: Major C. H. Pearce, Captain G. J. Scott, Lieutenant F. Green and Second-Lieutenant E. M. Thompson, April 1915.

George Purvis's original ***'battle cross'*** (that which marked his grave) hangs today on a pillar above the Green Howards Memorial Table in Bridlington's Priory Church as a tribute to him.

Second-Lieutenant J. S. Purvis, brother of G. B. Purvis, also served with the 5th Battalion. He survived the war and then entered the church. An accomplished artist, he became Rector of the Priory Church in Bridlington, before moving on to York as a Canon and archivist at York Minster.

Captain Frederick William Robson was promoted to Lieutenant-Colonel and later earned the Distinguished Service Order. He survived until killed in action on the 28th March 1918, aged thirty. Robson is commemorated on the Pozières Memorial, Pozières, France.

Lieutenant and Quartermaster Robert Rennison survived the war and went on to be a stalwart of the Old Comrades Association.

Lieutenant Thomas Ernest Dufty survived until killed in action on the 19th May 1915, while in the Hooge sector. He was 35. Dufty is buried at the Vlamertinghe Military Cemetery, Belgium, and is commemorated on the Bridlington War Memorial.

Lieutenant Frank Green survived until dying of his wounds on the 28th December 1917, sustained while in the Brandhoek area after a direct hit by an enemy shell on 'C' Company HQ. He was 23. Green is buried at the Lijssenhoek Military Cemetery, Belgium. The *'Casualty Listing'* for the 5th Battalion gives Green's rank as 'Private', however, as there is no corresponding service number given it is possible this is an error.

Lieutenant G. A. Maxwell is not listed as died.

Lieutenant Edward Reginald Spofforth survived until killed in action on the 2nd March 1916, while engaged in an attack on 'The Bluff'. He was 24. Spofforth is buried at the Poperinghe New Military Cemetery, Belgium.

Lieutenant J. S. Wadsworth is not listed as died.

Lieutenant Frank Woodcock was promoted to Captain and survived until killed in action on the 15th September 1916, while on the Somme. He was 22. Woodcock was the brother-in-law of Major Mortimer who was also killed on the Somme. He is buried at the Flatiron Copse Cemetery, Somme, France.

Second-Lieutenants A. F. Clarke, H. S. Cranswick, F. J. Dymond, G. Thomson and D. P. Tonks are not listed as died.

Bandsman Allan Parkinson, one of three brothers to serve with the 5th Battalion, all of them Bandsmen and therefore stretcher-bearers at the front. He died of his wounds on the 28th April 1916.

Second-Lieutenant Edward Medford Thompson was promoted to Lieutenant and survived until killed in action on the 26th February 1916, while supervising trench repairs in the Ypres sector. He was 28. Thompson is buried at the Poperinghe New Military Cemetery, Belgium. [There are three differing dates of Thompson's death, 22nd, 26th and 27th, recorded in different accounts. My Grandfather records it in his diary as the 26th, and as he was closest to the event I accept his date as being correct.]

Second-Lieutenant Wilfred Vause was promoted to Captain and earned the Military Cross. He survived until killed in action on the 23rd April 1917, while engaged on an attack during the Second Battle of the Scarpe. He was 27. Vause is buried at the Wancourt British Cemetery, Pas de Calais, France.

68 Bandsman Allan Parkinson was born in Scarborough and enlisted there. He was one of three brothers who served with the Territorials before the war in the 5th Green Howards Band, as did their uncles. Allan, a stretcher-bearer, survived until he died of his wounds - *'gunshot wounds right leg, right arm and compound fracture to the buttocks'* - at precisely 7.10pm on the 28th April 1916, while in the Dickebusch area. He was 21. Alan is buried at the Etaples Military Cemetery, Pas de Calais, France, and is commemorated on the Scarborough War Memorial.

The *'Casualty Listing'* for the 5th Battalion gives Allan's age as 37, however, I am assured by close friends of the family that his birth certificate shows his year of birth as 1895. This would have made him just 21 when he died.

241014 Bandsman Charles Parkinson, the eldest of the Parkinson brothers, also served with the 5th Battalion and survived the war, despite being wounded twice. In April 1919, aged 30, he was at Mulgrave Castle near Whitby, a hospital run by the Marquis and Marchioness of Normanby, among a group of wounded men who had formerly been prisoners of war - he was to suffer for the rest of his days with the problems caused by 'trench-foot' [a severe form of frost-bite]. After his father's retirement he took over and ran the family plumbing business and was a stalwart of the Old Comrades Association. He died in Scarborough on the 25th February 1963, aged 74.

Bandsman Simpson Parkinson appears to have had a most chequered time of it through the war. At the outbreak he served with

Former 5th Battalion Green Howards Bandsman Simpson Parkinson, pictured at home (above) with his sister, Lilian, wearing the cap badge of the Middlesex Regiment. Below: Simpson Parkinson (right) with sister Lilian (second left), Charles's wife, Charles and their son, pictured in Charles's back yard, Scarborough.

the 5th Battalion, with his brothers, but appears to have been drafted to other regiments each time he was wounded, serving with the East Surreys, the Cambridgeshire Regiment and the 1st Middlesex Regiment as part of a Lewis gun section. He survived the war, though lost a leg. Later he visited his brother Allan's grave and sent home a very descriptive letter for the benefit of his mother who could not travel there and see it for herself. Simpson, a member of the British Limbless Ex-Service Men's Association (BLESMA) died in Blackpool on the 24th February 1979, aged 85.

Private Charles Stamper Armstrong is not listed as died.

Chaplain, the Reverend B. Wolferstan earned the Military Cross and survived the war. He settled in St Helen's, Lancashire.

The Scarborough War Memorial,
unveiled on 26th September 1923,
was designed by Borough Engineer, Harold Smith,
and cost over £5,000, paid for by public subscription.

Epilogue

Following the war the Regiment earned, by dint of its Battalions' Great War service, the right to be called, simply, **The Green Howards**. It was officialdom's way of recognising their huge debt to Yorkshire's finest, the notification of which came in Army Order 509, published in 1920.

After the Great War, when the lads had done their bit and come marching home to ***'a land fit for heroes'***, reunions of the old comrades of regiments, battalions and units were commonplace. The 5th Green Howards were no exception and the Old Comrades Association was born; the date set for their anniversary was the 18th April, the day they first set foot in France, with their annual dinner set for St George's Day, the day they went into action.

Membership of the Association was strictly limited to those who had served overseas with the 5th Battalion during the Great War, including all attached details of the Royal Army Medical Corps, Royal Army Ordnance Corps, Royal Army Service Corps and the Army Chaplain Department. All those men who joined the 5th Green Howards, but who were posted overseas to other units were also eligible. The objects of the Association were to perpetuate the memory of the fallen, to promote true comradeship of the living and to instil principles of patriotism and loyalty in the young. The rules stated that an Annual Dinner be held on St George's Day to commemorate the Battalion's ***'baptism of fire'***, until such time as there was only one member left to drink a toast to the dead.

On the 26th September 1923, following a sombre procession through the town, the route of which was thronged with local people, the Scarborough War Memorial was unveiled before local dignitaries and one of the largest crowds of townsfolk ever seen. After the main unveiling of the memorial by the Chairman of the War Memorial Committee, Councillor William Boyes, the four 'faces' bearing the twelve bronze plaques of names, were unveiled by representatives of the Army, Navy, Royal Air Force and the Widows. The honour of representing the Army was given to Private Harold Merryweather of

The striking Canadian War Memorial at St Julien, near Ypres.

"This column marks the battlefield
where 18,000 Canadians,
on the British left,
withstood the first German gas-attack,
on 22nd-24th April 1915.
Two thousand fell and here lie buried."

the 5th Green Howards, one of the original Battalion who had landed in France in April 1915.

The obelisk-style Memorial, designed by Borough Engineer Harold W. Smith and paid for by public subscription to the tune of £5,000, was deliberately situated on the commanding promontory of Oliver's Mount, some five-hundred feet above sea-level, where it was, and remains today, visible from almost every part of the town. Built in hardy Yorkshire stone the Memorial bore the names of the fallen, both military and civilian, with part of the main inscription reading:

> *In grateful memory of the men of Scarborough who gave their lives for King and Country in the Great war, 1914-1919. They were a wall unto us both by night and day.*

The date of 1919 referred not to the Armistice of 11th November 1918, which many regarded as the war's end, but to the 'official' end of the war on 19th July 1919.

In 1924 members of Scarborough's Old Comrades Association once more returned to the battlefields of the Western Front, now silent and at peace, over which they had fought so hard for over 44 months. An account of their visit was written for the local paper by Lieutenant (QM) Robert Rennison (Lieutenant and Quartermaster in 1915).

> *Friday:*
> *This evening we visited the 49th (West Riding) Division Memorial at Essex Farm.*
>
> *Saturday:*
> *Today our tour was through Dickebusch, where there is nothing now to be seen of the huts or the Canadian lines. We went on through La Clytte to Scherpenburgh Hill and Locre, where we visited some of our old Billets and the place the Quarter-master had his stores. The church here is nearly finished being rebuilt. From there we went on to Outersteen, and there we found some of the people who were there in 1916, in the same places as they were at that time - although, of course,*

The imposing Menin Gate Memorial at Ypres, Belgium. The monument was designed by Sir Reginald Blomfield and was unveiled by Field Marshal Lord Plumer in 1927. It stands as a memorial to the 56,000 British troops who fell in the Ypres Salient prior to 6th August 1917, but who have no known graves.
The 5th Green Howards were no strangers to this part of war ravaged Ypres.

they are now rebuilt. The people at the Estaminet du Commerce were very pleased to see us, and remembered the days when 'C' Company were there.

At La Helle Croix the old people remembered Mr P. Foord, and one of our party found his brother's grave at the local cemetery. We stopped at Pont-de-Nieppe where the stone bridge leading to Armentières was destroyed and is now being built on a steel structure. Armentières is very advanced in rebuilding, except that Notre Dame Church in the Place de la Republique is badly destroyed and has not been touched.

An addition was made to our itinerary and we went on to Lille. We drove around the city and found it very busy - the centre is as busy as London. The city does not appear much damaged and there are many beautiful buildings there.

We got back to the hotel after a trip of some eight hours - while some of our party left us to visit the battlefields of Arras and the Somme.

Sunday:
We left the hotel this morning at 9.30am for a very interesting tour, for we went on to St Jean and St Julien.

There we saw the Canadian monument, where 18,000 Canadians withstood the first gas attack of the war. This is a very beautiful column with a Canadian soldier on the top. At Poelcapelle we found a very large cemetery, but only one of our own buried there. In all there are 8,000 men buried here, and 75% are unknown British soldiers. It is very touching to go around such a cemetery and to see the care bestowed on the graves.

We went on to the Passchendaele Ridge and Zonnebeke. In this district there are still a good many German pill-boxes. We went to Hooge,

The memorial to the fallen of the 50th (Northumbrian) Division at Wieltje, on the Ypres to St Julien road, was unveiled by Field Marshal Viscount Plumer on 1st September 1929.

Sanctuary Wood and Maple Copse, and also visited the Canadian memorial on Hill 62 - this is a lovely laid out spot, with gardens and terraces, and is marked 'Canada 1916'. We also visited Tyne Cot Cemetery where 13,000 soldiers are buried.

Sanctuary Wood was most interesting as it is still in the war condition. The wastage of war is still visible, and the trenches are to be seen, although there is a lot of undergrowth. Several members of the party were able to visualise what the battlefields had been like when they had walked over some of the actual ground over which the 5th Green Howards had fought, with rifles, bombs, equipment and dug-out material lying about everywhere.

We came back to the hotel via Hell Fire Corner, having found many of our comrades' graves in the various cemeteries. Some of the party had not yet had enough and so went off to Lille.

Monday:
On Monday we visited Vlamertinghe, Poperinghe and Ouderdorn, and at all these places found the graves of many of our fallen comrades. At Vlamertinghe there are 1,200 men buried and the cemetery is well kept, full of flowers and roses.

It was not until 1929 that a memorial to the fallen of the 50th (Northumbrian) Division was unveiled. Suitably, it was situated on the Ypres to St Julien road. The newspapers of the time noted the event.

UNVEILING OF THE MEMORIAL

Field Marshal Viscount Plumer is to unveil the memorial in honour of the officers, NCOs and men of the 50th (Northumbrian) Division, who fell in the Great War. The memorial has been erected at Wieltje, on the Ypres-St Julien road. It takes the

The Eleanor Cross at Sledmere, near Driffield, to which Sir Mark Sykes added brasses and plaques dedicated to his comrades of the 5th Green Howards. Fifty yards away is the Waggoners Memorial.

form of a severely plain, but impressive, stone obelisk, about 55 feet high, designed by Captain R. Mauchlen, MC, late of the 9th Durham Light Infantry, and immediately overshadows Oxford Road British Cemetery, with only a field of flax dividing it from the wayside. 'God's Acre' wherein are buried 404 soldiers of the United Kingdom, 74 Canadians, 73 Australians, 37 New Zealanders, 9 Newfoundlanders, 2 Guernsey Militia and 248 'unknown' soldiers of the British Empire.

The Northumbrian Division, which included various units from Northumberland, Durham, Yorkshire, Lancashire, Cumberland and Ayrshire, first went into action at Wieltje, and from 1915 to 1918 our front line held the village, the line extending along 'Oxford Road' and thence down 'Cambridge Road' to 'Birr Cross Roads'.

One of our largest dug-outs, capable of holding 300 men, was situated in 'Admiralty Road' facing the north side of the memorial; while at Railway Wood, on 'Cambridge Road' stands the monument to those gallant tunnellers who endured 30 months of continuous underground warfare.

MEMORIALS INSIGNIA & INSCRIPTIONS

The North Face

Head of the White Horse of Northumbria with an up-pointed sword, graven in stone beneath. Below, the words, 'To the enduring memory of all ranks of the 50th Northumbrian Division, who fell in the Great War, 1914-1918. Pro Patris'.

~

The West Face

149th Infantry Brigade:

4th, 5th, 6th, 7th Northumberland Fusiliers (TF)

5th Border Regiment (TF)

150th Infantry Brigade:

The 4th Battalion (to which the survivors of the 5th Battalion were posted) being presented to Lord Middleton at Bridlington after the war by Captain Lofthouse (himself a former POW). Very few of the 'original' 5th Battalion survived this far.

4th East Yorkshire Regiment (TF)
4th, 5th Yorkshire Regiment (TF)
[the Green Howards]
5th Durham Light Infantry (TF)
151st Infantry Brigade:
6th, 7th, 8th Durham Light Infantry (TF)
5th Loyal North Lancashire Regiment (TF)

~

The East Face
Ayrshire Yeomanry
Yorkshire Hussars
1st, 2nd, 3rd, 4th Northumbrian Brigade Royal Field Artillery (TF)
Northumbrian Ammunition Column (TF)
Northumbrian Divisional Engineers of the Royal Engineers
50th Divisional Train of the Royal Army Service Corps
1st, 2nd, 3rd Northumbrian Field Ambulance, Royal Army Medical Corps (TF)
Northumbrian Divisional Casualty Clearing Station (TF)
Northumbrian Veterinary Section, Royal Army Veterinary Corps (TF)
Royal Army Ordnance Corps

~

Two seats of hard blue Belgian stone have been provided on the east and west sides respectively, and yew trees have been planted at the four corners of the memorial.

The '*Head of the White Horse*' referred to above was in fact the head of a unicorn, the personal crest of Major General Sir Percival Wilkinson [Colonel of the Northumberland Fusiliers from 1915 to 1935] who commanded the 50th Division from August 1915 to February 1918. However, the Unicorn was replaced as the Divisional Sign of the 50th Division during the Second World War with the familiar double T symbol; the second T being '*dropped*' slightly and overlapping the first T.

The Battle Honours of the Green Howards.

In 1937 some 250 members of the Old Comrades Association came together for their 16th annual reunion. On that occasion the Reverend J. S. Purvis addressed his old comrades before the Bridlington Cenotaph, and expressed his concern over the younger generation's seeming indifference to the sacrifices made by those fallen men of the Great War.

> *They have grown up in a world constantly overshadowed by the fear, and threat, and rumour of war, and yet we had no idea of being involved in a war until 1914 came. They may think that you men come here today to keep alive something of that spirit of militarism which is seen in the boastfulness of certain foreign nations today, or that we went overseas in 1914 in the modern spirit of aggressive nationalism. That is not so. We had not foreseen war in 1914, we had not intended war, and we did not desire it. But a call came where so far as we, and these, our dead comrades could see there was only one course which a man could take if he valued honesty, and justice, and loyalty to his country as the best things which he knew. They had to set these things against the chance that they might have to give their lives, and though they loved peace and loved their homes, they did not hesitate. War is a vile thing. Not one of you will deny that, and you know something about it. But these men faced it, and gave their lives for what they believed right. Let no man dare to speak of them with anything but reverence. We are here today, as for so many years past, to do them honour for their sacrifice, and to remember the things to which they were prepared to be faithful, even unto death.*

The Comrades continued to hold their annual reunions, even during the years of the Second World War when a number of them served their country again; though inevitably, over the years, their numbers thinned.

The Great War Battle Honours of The Green Howards (Alexandra, Princess of Wales's Own Yorkshire Regiment)

YPRES 1914, 1915, 1917
Langemarck 1914, 1917, Gheluvelt, Neuve Chapelle, St Julien, Frezenberg, Bellewaarde, Aubers Festubert 1915
LOOS
SOMME 1916, 1918
Albert 1916, Bazentin, Pozières, Flers-Courcelette, Morval, Thiepval, Le Transloy, Ancre Heights, Ancre 1916
ARRAS 1917, 1918
Scarpe 1917, 1918
MESSINES 1917, 1918
Pilckem, Menin Road, Polygon Wood, Broodseinde, Poelcappelle, Passchendaele, Cambrai 1917, 1918, St Quentin, Bapaume 1918, Rosières, Lys, Estaires, Hazebrouck, Kemmel, Scherpenberg, Aisne 1918, Drocourt-Quèant, Hindenburg Line, Canal du Nord, Beaurevoir, Selle
VALENCIENNES
SAMBRE
FRANCE AND FLANDERS 1914-1918
Piave
VITTORIO VENETO
Italy 1917-1918
SULVA
Landing at Sulva, Scimitar Hill, Gallipoli 1915, Egypt 1916, Archangel 1918

On Friday the 26th October 1945 the then 5th Green Howards were paraded in Scarborough as the Freedom of the Borough was bestowed upon the Regiment. With swords drawn, bayonets fixed, their Colours streaming in the wind, the Battalion marched to the beat of the drums, the sound of their boots echoing through the streets where once had marched the men of an earlier generation, the men of the first 5th Battalion. As those veterans stood among the crowds and watched - the same men who believed they had fought ***'the war to end all wars'*** - one can't help but wonder how many had shaken their heads, with a lump in the throat and a tear in the eye for the memory of fallen comrades, and quietly swore to themselves, *'pray God never again'*. Since then the Regiment has also been granted the honour of the Freedom of Richmond, Middlesbrough, Redcar, Bridlington and Beverley.

At the 1946 reunion of the Old Comrades, the Mayor of Scarborough, Alderman J. Jackson was the principal speaker and it was with pride that he spoke of those first days of action in April 1915. He told how he had received a letter from his eldest son, serving with the 5th Green Howards, written on the 25th April 1915, in which he described the bullets coming through the trees when they got the order to ***'move off'***. That same night his son had been killed, and he had always felt proud that one of his sons had died for his country in a regiment like the Green Howards. Later he had been sent his son's medals and, pausing dramatically, he had opened his coat and revealed the medals to the hushed assembly.

> *They have never been uncovered up to today, but tonight I have put them on my right breast in honour of my son and to let you see that I am proud of them.*

In 1966 those Old Comrades who remained were guests of honour at the Scarborough Freedom March of the Green Howards when the Regiment exercised its right to the 'Freedom' of the Borough.

Over the years their numbers steadily dwindled, and eventually the annual reunion ended; the 18th April, with few left to remember it, finally settled into the dust as a mere footnote in history.

With the death of Scarborian Jim Stevenson, on 26th May 1996, the very last of the original 5th Battalion - those who landed in France in

Jim Stevenson - the last of the original 5th Battalion's 'Yorkshire Gurkhas' - 3rd April 1996, with Drummer Peter Hughes and Private Lee Miller.

April 1915 - has gone. Had it not been for the careful storage of his diaries, letters and photographs, as well as his vivid and lucid memories, none of this would have been written, for it was he who kindled my interest and thirst for knowledge.

I must confess that throughout the research and writing of this book I have all too often been moved to tears by the stout-hearted way these young men bore their lot, toiling through such great adversity often with a smile and a song. Only the heart of the most arrogant and jaundiced individual could fail to be moved by their great sacrifice. It is abundantly clear to me, after speaking to the many people who have contacted me following my numerous appeals for information, that none of these brave men will ever be forgotten.

I hope that in years to come some of you may join with me on St George's Day, in spirit if not in person, in raising a glass of remembrance to the 5th Green Howards.

This work stands as a small testament to the strength and noble courage of the men who were the heart and soul of the 5th Green Howards, those never-before warriors; Terriers, justly honoured by their own comrades-in-arms as the ***'Yorkshire Gurkhas'***.

May each and every one of them rest in peace.

Mark Marsay
Scarborough
February 1999

The Green Howards Territorials ~ A CONCISE HISTORY ~

This book recounts the deeds of the Scarborough-based Territorials at the Second Battle of Ypres over eighty years ago. But it is worth noting that the 5th Green Howards enjoy a long and distinguished record of volunteer soldiering, one which is second to none in today's Territorial Army. The unit's continuous service spans nearly 130 years, both in peacetime and in three major wars, right up to the present day.

Scarborough's Volunteers were raised as Rifle Volunteers in 1860 to counter the invasion threat of France's Emperor, Napoleon III. They were then designated as the ***6th Yorkshire (North Riding) Rifle Volunteer Corps*** of the new Volunteer Force (VF). In company with all such units their uniforms, equipment, arms and drill halls were paid for from their own pockets.

In 1883 the British Infantry of the Line was finally completing a reorganisation into a new system of 'County' regiments. This resulted in the district's Rifle Volunteer Corps being re-designated as the ***2nd Volunteer Battalion The Princess of Wales's Own (Yorkshire Regiment) (VF)*** with battalion headquarters and companies at North Street, Scarborough, and additional companies in the outlying districts. This same re-designation brought Scarborough's volunteers into the Green Howards, whose regimental title they now bore; at the same time Northallerton's Rifle Volunteers became the 1st Volunteer Battalion.

In 1899 the British regular army suffered three disastrous defeats whilst fighting the Boers in South Africa. This led to Volunteer Force battalions providing Active Service Companies to fight in South Africa as part of their respective regular battalions. The deeds of Scarborough's volunteers on active service in South Africa were subsequently recognised by the award of the Battalion's first battle honour - ***'South Africa 1900-1902'***.

The old Volunteer Force was reorganised in 1908 to become the **Territorial Force (TF)** and Scarborough's 2nd Volunteer Battalion was re-designated ***5th Battalion Alexandra Princess of Wales's Own Yorkshire Regiment (TF)***. This reorganisation also brought to the 5th Battalion a number of companies from the former 2nd Volunteer Battalion The East Yorkshire Regiment (VF). One of these was the Driffield Company whose Commander, **Captain James Mortimer**, had served with the Volunteer Active Service Company in South Africa and who was destined to command the 5th Battalion in 1915. Northallerton's 1st Volunteer Battalion was concurrently re-designated as the 4th Battalion.

1908 also witnessed the formation of the wholly Territorial Force ***Northumbrian Division*** which was in time to earn a deserved reputation as one of the finest divisions in the British Army. The Green Howards' 4th and 5th Battalions (TF), and Hull's 4th Battalion The East Yorkshire Regiment (TF) joined with the 5th Durham Light Infantry (TF), Stockton-on-Tees, to form ***The York and Durham Brigade***, beginning an association which would see them fighting side-by-side in two world wars.

The 5th Green Howards were rushed back from annual camp in North Wales to be embodied for war in August 1914. So many former Territorials and new recruits flocked to join the battalion that a nucleus of experienced officers and men was detailed to form a Second-Line **'2/5th Battalion'**, which was in due course to furnish reinforcement drafts for the original battalion, which was now re-designated as the **'1/5th'**. The 1/5th Battalion saw active service in France and Flanders, from 1915 to 1918, as part of the ***150th (1st York and Durham) Infantry Brigade***.

The 1/5th Battalion's final battle was in May 1918 on the Marne when its 150th Brigade was violently attacked by a vastly superior German force during which the Green Howards held their line and literally fought to the last round before being inevitably overwhelmed.

The 5th Battalion was reconstituted in 1920 when the Territorial Army came into being. In line with a change in the Regiment's title it was now designated ***5th Battalion The Green Howards (Alexandra, Princess of Wales's Own Yorkshire Regiment) (TA)***.

In 1938 the 50th (Northumbrian) Division became a 'motor division', of two brigades, (150th and 151st Brigades) with the role of supporting armour. As the prospect of war loomed in 1939 the Territorial Army was instructed to double in strength and the 5th Battalion divided to form the ***5th Battalion (150th Brigade)*** and a new ***7th Battalion (69th Brigade)***, based on its Bridlington company. Similarly the ***4th Battalion (150th Brigade)*** divided and raised the ***6th Battalion (69th Brigade)***.

The 4th and 5th Battalions again served with the 150th Brigade, 50th Division, in World War II and first saw active service in north-west Europe in 1940, as did their duplicate battalions (6th and 7th) of the 69th Brigade.

Green Howards' Territorials were amongst the last to leave the Dunkirk beaches and the 50th Division put in the only British counter-attack of the whole campaign.

The 50th Division then reverted to being a three brigade division by the addition of the 69th Brigade (69th, 150th and 151st Brigades).

The division moved to North Africa in 1941 and was soon engaged in desert warfare against Rommel's German Africa Corps. In May 1942 the 4th and 5th Green Howards formed part of the ***'150th Brigade Box'*** at Got El Ualeb which became surrounded by several of Rommel's Divisions. The Green Howards fought a battle which Rommel later described as the toughest defence he encountered in the whole of the desert war. With no hope of reinforcement, and desperately outnumbered, the Green Howards were finally encircled and over-run.

The 6th and 7th Green Howards continued the struggle in North Africa, Sicily and in Normandy.

Few divisions, if any, equalled the fighting record of the 50th (Northumbrian) Division in World War II - certainly none excelled it.

The 5th Green Howards re-formed with a new role in 1947 under the designation ***631st (Green Howards) Anti-Tank Regiment Royal Artillery (TA)***.

In 1948 Battalion Headquarters moved to Coldyhill Lane, Scarborough.

And in 1961 the Battalion amalgamated with the 4th Battalion to form the ***4th/5th Battalion The Green Howards (Alexandra, Princess of Wales's Own Yorkshire Regiment) (TA)***.

Between 1967 and 1993 the Battalion was represented by Green Howards' Companies of the ***Yorkshire Volunteers*** until being re-designated in 1993 as the familiar ***4th/5th Battalion The Green Howards (Alexandra, Princess of Wales's Own Yorkshire Regiment) (Yorkshire Volunteers)***.

The 4th/5th Battalion today has headquarters in Middlesbrough with company drill halls across the North Riding.

Today's Territorials are undoubtedly proud of their forebears, not least those of the ***'old 5th Battalion'*** who in 1915 proved beyond doubt that Scarborough's Saturday Night Soldiers were more than worthy members of an outstanding Yorkshire Regiment.

Major Tony Podmore, MBE, TD
Horsforth, Leeds
February 1999

AUTHOR'S NOTE

As this book went to press the details of the recent Strategic Defence Review were becoming known and the huge impact on the Territorial Army felt.

The 4th/5th Battalion has not escaped unscathed. It is to be disbanded as a battalion on 31st March 1999. However, two of its companies, those based at Scarborough ('A' Company) and Middlesbrough ('B' Company), are to form part of the new North East Battalion, based in Durham (which comes into being on 1st July 1999), which will also comprise two companies of the 6th Royal Regiment of Fusiliers (from Ashington and Newcastle) and one company from the 7th Light Infantry - what was the Durham Light Infantry - (from Bishop Auckland). The Headquarters of the 4th/5th Green Howards, at Coulby Newham, Middlesbrough is to be disbanded and its premises handed over to other units, while 'C' Company based at Harrogate, and the Guisborough and Northallerton Detachments are all to be disbanded.

For the foreseeable future each company of the new North East Battalion will wear its own Regimental cap badge, but no one can say if this will be long term.

It appears, once again, as if the days of the Green Howards Terriers are numbered.

Sincere thanks and acknowledgements go to:

Lieutenant-Colonel Neil McIntosh, MBE, of the Green Howards Regimental Headquarters, Major (Retired) Roger Chapman, MBE, and the redoubtable Steve Rarity of the Green Howards Regimental Museum, Richmond, North Yorkshire, for invaluable assistance with research and for permission to reproduce material from their archives and Regimental and Battalion records.

The Editor of the Scarborough Evening News (Yorkshire Regional Newspapers) for permission to reproduce material from *'The Scarborough Pictorial'*, 1914-1918, and for printing my appeal for information on the men of the 5th Green Howards.

E. T. W. Dennis and Sons for permission to reproduce material from the 1915 souvenir booklet *'The German Raid on Scarborough'*.

For printing my appeal for information on the 50th Division; The Editor of the Yorkshire Post and The Editor of the Northern Echo (also for permission to reproduce material).

The following branches of the Green Howards Association, for their help, advice and encouragement with this book: Scarborough Branch - George Wilson and Gerry Coates; Bridlington Branch - Mark Major; Malton Branch - Philip Banbury.

Note: *sadly, Mark Major died before this book was published. He was a personal friend and was constant in his support and encouragement of my research and work. Mark was a gentleman in every sense of the word and he will be sorely missed.*

Sir Tatton Sykes and Colonel A. Wilson for their assistance with the biographical details of Sir Mark Sykes.

For their permission to reproduce material; Rita Raper (niece of Private B. Watson); Betty Rose (daughter of Captain E. H. Weighill and daughter-in-law of Lieutenant L. H. Rose); Alan Richmond (grandson of Private H. Richmond); Joyce Whitehead (daughter of Colonel C. H. Pearce); Susan Stobart (daughter of Major R. M. Gladstone); Shirley Langdale (close friend of the Parkinson family); Charles Monkman (son of Private C. Monkman) and Roger Price.

Tonie and Valmai Holt for permission to reproduce Bruce Bairnsfather material.

Ray Westlake for his assistance and encouragement.

Captain Brian Hemmerman for help with the 150th Field Ambulance.

Ken Campbell for help with the Malton men of the Battalion.

The staffs of the Reference Section of Scarborough Library, Ayton village Library and Malton town Library.

The Ayton Women's Institute, for details of the Barber Memorial Trees.

The staff of the Commonwealth War Graves Commission for the *'Casualty Listing'* of the 5th Battalion.

Ray, Joan and Steve Flint for their support.

Those many generous folk, both far and wide, who have responded to my appeals and shared of their precious store of memories and mementos - all of which will be used in subsequent works.

And last, but by no means least my *'trio'* of ladies; my dear old Mum, Shirley for her constant encouragement, my Aunt Sybil for her support, and my long-suffering wife Diane - who spent many long hours checking the numerous drafts, who made endless cups of coffee in the wee small hours and who stood resolute throughout the many setbacks.

Special Acknowledgements

It is only right that I single out for a special acknowledgement Tony Podmore, not only for his diligent checking of the various drafts of the manuscript, but for putting up with me picking his brains, asking questions and raising queries, *answering them all,* and for supplying and allowing me to use, without compunction, the fruits of his own considerable labours, research and writing. I thank him for his enthusiasm and encouragement throughout - his ready and evident pride in the Territorial Army and its history and origins has benefited this work considerably.

The publication of this work would have been impossible without the considerable financial support of my father-in-law, Gordon Richard Crowther, who died suddenly and tragically in November 1997, aged just 58. A man with an enormous appetite for life, I am sure he would have been proud to see the fruition of many years of hard work and the dream realised.

Main Reference Material

Wylly, Colonel H. C., *The Green Howards in the Great War*, Privately Printed, 1926.
Tovey & Podmore, Colonel W. J. and Major A. J., *Once a Howard - Twice a Citizen*, Volunteers Press, 1995.
Wyrall, E., *The History of the 50th Division*, Lund Humphires, 1939.
Powell, Colonel G., *The History of the Green Howards - 300 Years of Service*, Arms & Armour, 1992.
Jarvis, S. D. & D. B, *The Cross of Sacrifice Volume 1, Officers who died in the service of British, Indian and East African Regiments and Corps 1914-1919*, Roberts Medals, 1993.
Pope & Wheal, S. and E. A., *The Macmillan Dictionary of the First World War*, Macmillan, 1995.
James, Brigadier E. A., *British Regiments 1914-1918*, Naval and Military Press, 1993.
Banbury, Major P., *The Sledmere Cross* (unpublished), 1996.
Thompson, B., *The Great War dead of Ayton* (unpublished), 1986.
Ayton Women's Institute, *The History of Ayton*, Privately Printed, Ayton Women's Institute.
Stevenson, J. R., *Accumulated diaries and papers* (unpublished).
Swinton, Major General Sir Ernest, *Twenty Years After*, Newnes, 1938.
Holt, T. and V., *In Search of a Better 'Ole*, Milestone, 1985.
Adelson, R., *Mark Sykes - Portrait of an Amateur*, J. Cape, 1975.

Scarborough Pictorial for the period 1914-1918.
The German Raid on Scarborough, E. T. W. Dennis and Sons, 1915.
The Official History of the Great War, France and Belgium 1915, Volume 1, Imperial War Museum/Battery Press, 1995.
Officers died in the Great War, 1914-1919, Hayward & Son, 1988.
Soldiers died in the Great War, 1914-1919, Hayward & Son, 1989.
Battle Honours awarded for the Great War, Ray Westlake, 1992.

PHOTOGRAPHS AND ILLUSTRATIONS

Pages: v, xviii, 8, 10, 16, 18, 20, 24, 26, 28, 30, 32, 34, 36, 40, 42, 72, 94, 164, 166, 168, 176
 - *Author's Collection*
Pages: 2, 48, 52, 56, 58, 60, 66, 78, 82, 84, 86, 88, 96, 100, 104, 108, 110, 112, 114, 116, 118, 120, 124, 128, 136, 142, 146, 148, 150, 154, 156
 - *Scarborough Pictorial (Yorkshire Regional Newspapers)*
Pages: 4, 6
 - *E. T. W. Dennis & Sons*
Pages: 12, 14, 38
 - *'20 Years After'*
Pages: 22 and 170
 - *'History of the 50th Division'*
Pages: 46, 62, 68, 92, 102, 118 top, 140, 152, 174
 - *The Green Howards Regimental Museum*
Pages: 50 top, 54
 - *Charles Monkman*
Page: 50 bottom
 - *Rita Raper*
Pages: 64, 90
 - *Susan Stobart*
Pages: 70, 74, 106, 126, 132, 138, 144, 158
 - *Joyce Whitehead*
Page: 76
 - *Roger Price*
Pages: 80, 98
 - *Alan Richmond*
Page: 122
 - *Betty Rose*
Pages: 160, 162 top and bottom
 - *Shirley Langdale*
Page: 172
 - *Philip Banbury*
Page: 180
 - *Northern Echo*

CORRECTIONS ~ OMISSIONS

Although every effort has been made to verify facts and figures given in this work it is quite possible there will be some errors. If notified of errors in the text, the author will undertake to correct them for any future editions and any subsequent works. Notice of correction can be forwarded via the publishers.

MAIL ORDER & DISCOUNTS

Further copies of this book are available at £7.99 each, postage and packing free, from the address at the foot of the page. Please make cheques payable to 'Great Northern Publishing'. Discounts are available for trade, retail and bulk purchasing, please write for details.

If you would like to receive notification of our books as they are published, please forward your details to the address below and we will be pleased to add you to our mailing list.

NOTE: Once on our mail order list you will be offered substantial discounts - up to 25% off marked prices in most cases.

As a small, independent, regional publisher we are always happy to hear what our readers think about our books and endeavour to reply to all correspondence, so please feel free to drop us a line.

ADVERTISING

Great Northern Publishing welcomes discreet advertising in its books. Any business or company who would like further details is invited to contact us at the address below.

PRODUCTION SERVICE

Great Northern Publishing ***does not*** accept unsolicited manuscripts, but does offer a fully comprehensive production service for authors, charities and organisations who are considering, or wish to 'self-publish' their work (this includes all types of books, magazines, newsletters, brochures etc). This is a professional service and should not be mistaken for 'vanity publishing' or 'joint venture publishing'. For further details please send a first class s.a.e. to the address below.

GREAT NORTHERN PUBLISHING
PO Box 202, Scarborough, North Yorkshire YO11 3GE

AUTHOR'S APPEAL

For the first time, the full story of the 4th and 5th Green Howards Terriers in the Great War is being told in print.

This book, 'Baptism of Fire', is the first in several planned volumes and to that end the author would be extremely grateful to hear from anyone who has any material about either battalion from the period 1914-1919.

The Green Howards (The Yorkshire Regiment) recruited men from a very large geographic area - from the Humber to the Tyne and from north to west coast. Of special interest are the personal diaries, photographs, letters, postcards and verse of the men who served. If you can help with the loan (material will be returned as soon as possible), or donation of such material for copying etc., please contact the author by letter in the first instance via the offices of the publisher (address below). Once used, all the material donated will be deposited in the archives of the Green Howards Regimental Museum, Richmond, North Yorkshire.

Those who died are recorded on monuments or graves both here and in France and Belgium, but for those Terriers who *returned* from the Western Front there is no monument. It is the author's hope that these volumes will rectify that, before the memory of these brave men passes away forever.

GREAT NORTHERN PUBLISHING
PO Box 202
Scarborough
North Yorkshire
YO11 3GE

Index

Page numbers in bold italics, ***55*** thus, denote photographs and maps

T

V

W

Y

Z

Other Units Mentioned (not in order):

2nd and 4th Green Howards
5th, 6th, 7th, 8th and 9th Durham Light Infantry
3rd and 4th East Yorkshire Regiment
2nd Volunteer Battalion East Yorkshire Regiment
4th, 5th, 6th and 7th Northumberland Fusiliers
5th Border Regiment
5th Loyal North Lancashire Regiment
2nd Zouave Battalion
1st Princess Victoria's Royal Irish Rifles
2nd Battalion Montreal Canadian Division
18th Queen Mary's Own Hussars
3rd Canadian Infantry Brigade
13th Brigade
149th Brigade
150th Brigade
151st Brigade
50th (1st Northumbrian) Division
1st, 2nd, 3rd and 4th Northumbrian Brigade Royal Field Artillery
Northumbrian Ammunition Column
Northumbrian Divisional Engineers of the Royal Engineers
50th Divisional Train of the Royal Army Service Corps
1st, 2nd and 3rd Northumbrian Field Ambulance Royal Army Medical Corps
Northumbrian Divisional Casualty Clearing Station
Northumbrian Veterinary Section, Royal Army Veterinary Corps
Royal Army Ordnance Corps
4th Canadian Division
5th Division
28th Division
49th (West Riding) Division
Lahore Division
V Corps Reserve (Second Army)
The London Regiment
Royal Fusiliers
Seaforth Highlanders
Yorkshire Hussars Yeomanry, Alexandra, Princess of Wales's Own
East Surreys
Cambridgeshire Regiment
Middlesex Regiment
Ayrshire Yeomanry
Machine Gun Corps
Royal Inniskilling Fusiliers
Royal Garrison Artillery (TF)
10th Brigade (4th Canadian Division)
18th West Yorkshires
Nottinghamshire and Derbyshire Regiment
North Riding Regiment of Volunteers
Royal Flying Corps

Coming Soon, Mark Marsay's . . .

THE WAR OF

THE YORKSHIRE GURKHAS

THE FULL ACCOUNT OF THE 5TH GREEN HOWARDS
IN THE GREAT WAR ~ 1914 TO 1919

Told in several volumes, here is the only full and detailed account of the 5th Green Howards in the Great War. Using the personal diaries and memories of his late Grandfather, Private Jim Stevenson MM, the author has combined them with official records and documents to produce, for the first time in print, the war of the 'Yorkshire Gurkhas'.

From the outbreak of war in 1914, when the battalion was busy training in Wales, to 1918 when it was reduced to cadre status due to overwhelming losses and when many of its men were transferred to the 4th Green Howards (among them Private Stevenson MM), these volumes tell the Terriers' story.

Private Stevenson's diaries form the backbone to the whole work, including the battalion's Baptism of Fire at St Julien in 1915, the action on the Somme for which he was awarded the Military Medal, the night-time crater raid at Petit Bois, the occasions he was wounded and gassed, through his time as a Scout and a batman to two of the Battalion's finest officers and his eventual capture in 1918; when he became a prisoner of war and yet still managed to maintain a diary of events up to his eventual repatriation late in 1919.

If you have any material relating to the 4th or 5th Green Howards during the Great War, especially the diaries, letters and photographs of those who served, you are urgently invited to contact the author via the offices of the publisher at the address on page 201.

Readers Special Offer

VINTAGE MUSIC ON CD

ORIGINAL RECORDINGS FROM THE 20s, 30s AND 40s

BIX BEIDERBECKE
'AT THE JAZZ BAND BALL'
22 ORIGINAL RECORDINGS
1932-1938

Including:
Clementine
Davenport Blues
Fidgety Feet
For No Reason At All
From Monday On
Mississippi Mud
Tiger Rag
Way Down Yonder

GEORGE FORMBY
'WHEN I'M
CLEANING WINDOWS'
24 ORIGINAL RECORDINGS
1936-1940

Including:
Leaning On A Lamp-Post
My Plus Fours
Our Sergeant Major
They Can't Fool Me
Stick Of Blackpool Rock
I'm A Froggie
It's In The Air
Hill Billy Willie

FLANAGAN & ALLEN
'WE'LL SMILE AGAIN'
25 ORIGINAL RECORDINGS
1932-1944

Including:
Forget Me Not Lane
F. D. R. Jones
Underneath The Arches
Siegfried Line
Yesterday's Dreams
Home Town
Nice People
Dreaming

LOUIS ARMSTRONG
'HOT FIVES & HOT SEVENS'
25 ORIGINAL RECORDINGS
1926-1928

Including:
Heebie Jeebies
Savoy Blues
Weather Bird
West End Blues
Willie The Weeper
Jazz Lips
St James' Infirmary
Skid-Dat-De-Dat

CAB CALLOWAY
'KICKING THE
GONG AROUND'
20 ORIGINAL RECORDINGS
1930-1931

Including:
Aw, You Dog!
Bugle Call Rag
Minnie The Moocher
St Louis Blues
Swing It
Waltzing The Blues
When Lights Are Low
Lonesome Nights

OFFER CONTINUED OVERLEAF: